CHRISTOLOGY
AFTER AUSCHWITZ

CHRISTOLOGY
AFTER AUSCHWITZ

by
Michael B. McGarry, C.S.P.

PAULIST PRESS
New York/Ramsey/Toronto

Library of Congress
Catalog Card Number: 77-73977

ISBN: 0-8091-2024-0

Published by Paulist Press
Editorial Office: 1865 Broadway, New York, N.Y. 10023
Business Office: 545 Island Road, Ramsey, N.J. 07446

Printed and bound in the
United States of America

Acknowledgements

I would like to acknowledge those who have helped me prepare this book, particularly my professors Harry McSorley, Gregory Baum, and Alan Davies. Others, like Dan Donovan, Terry Forestell, and Bill Kondrath, in a more remote, but no less real, way inspired me to strive for careful thinking and research in theological studies; to them I am deeply grateful. While I am indebted to them for their help, I take full responsibility for the contents of this book.

My gratitude extends also to my community, the Paulists, who released me from other pastoral duties in order to complete this work, and to Carolyn Meeks who typed the manuscript.

Finally, to my parents I dedicate this book—it was they who first taught me that to believe in Jesus as Christ does not thereby invalidate others' responses as they remain faithful to their own call from God our Father.

Contents

Contents

I
Introduction:
Background and Statement
of the Issue

The horrors of Auschwitz still loom large in the minds and hearts of the Jewish people of the world. What could such an unprecedented, demonic event mean in the history of its survivors? Can there be meaning at all in such a catastrophe? If nothing else, Auschwitz has provoked many Jewish thinkers to a new, corporate rethinking of Judaism's meaning and survival.[1]

On the Christian side, theologians and Church leaders, in moments of contrition and bewilderment, wonder how such a catastrophe as the holocaust could have happened in a Christian country, in a nation nurtured and steeped in the Christian tradition.[2] Antisemitism,[3] to be sure, predates Christianity,[4] but

---

1. E.g., see Gregory Baum, "Theology after Auschwitz: A Conference Report," *The Ecumenist* 12 (1974):65-80; Eliezer Berkovits, *Faith After the Holocaust* (New York: KTAV Publishing House, 1973); Alice L. Eckardt, "The Holocaust: Christian and Jewish Responses," *Journal of the American Academy of Religion* 42 (1974):453-469; Richard L. Rubenstein, *After Auschwitz, Radical Theology and Contemporary Judaism* (Indianapolis: Bobbs-Merrill Co., Inc., 1966), *et al.*

2. See Franklin H. Littell, "Christendom, Holocaust and Israel: The Importance of Recent Major Events in Jewish History," *Journal of Ecumenical Studies* [hereafter *JES*] 10 (1973):483-497, who argues that the facts of the holocaust and of the state of Israel force Christians to change their teaching about Israel. Cf. also his *The Crucifixion of the Jews: The Failure of Christians To Understand the Jewish Experience* (New York: Harper and Row, 1975); Gregory Baum, "Introduction," to Rosemary Ruether's *Faith and Fratricide: The Theological Roots of Anti-Semitism* (New York: The Seabury Press, 1974), p. 8.

never before have men focused such a genocidal fury on the Jews with such an unambiguous goal—the annihilation of the Jewish people.[5]

In an effort to eradicate every form of, and justification for, antisemitism from Christianity, Church theologians and leaders have tried to investigate what could have laid the groundwork for such an expression of hate and utter disregard for human dignity.[6] Some, ashamed at their own Church's silence during the attempt at the "final solution," have pointed to the "unchristian behavior" of the Christian Church. That is, if Christians had been more truly faithful to the teachings of Christ, they never could have given in to the evils of antisemitism.

Others have suggested that the answer is deeper and more radical than a matter of moral behavior: the basis for antisemitism is to be found in the Scriptures themselves, or, if not in the New Testament, in the content of Church teaching and doc-

3. Following James Parkes: " 'Antisemitism' . . . is not a scientific word, entitling it to a hyphen, nor has it anything to do with something called 'Semitism,' entitling it to the capitals. It is a political term meaning 'Jew-hatred.' " From James Parkes, "Judaism and the Jewish People in Their World Setting at the End of 1973," pamphlet distributed by the Canadian Council of Christians and Jews (Toronto, 1974). For a definition of this term, we will follow Jules Isaac, *The Teaching of Contempt: Christian Roots of Anti-Semitism* (New York: Holt, Rinehart and Winston, 1964), p. 21: "Anti-Semitism is used nowadays to refer to anti-Jewish prejudice, to feelings of suspicion, contempt, hostility, and hatred towards Jews, both those who follow the religion of Israel and those who are merely of Jewish parentage."

4. For histories of antisemitism, see Edward Flannery, *The Anguish of the Jews* (New York: Macmillan, 1964); Jules Isaac, *The Teaching of Contempt*; Leon Poliakon, *The History of Anti-Semitism* (4 volumes) (New York: The Vanguard Press, 1965); James Parkes, *Antisemitism* (Chicago: Quadrangle Books, 1963); Rosemary Ruether, *Faith and Fratricide*, pp. 23-63; Alan Davies, *Anti-Semitism and the Christian Mind: The Crisis of Conscience after Auschwitz* (New York: Herder and Herder, 1969), pp. 23-34; *et al*.

5. For the most comprehensive account of the single-mindedness and execution of the Hitler regime concerning the Jews, see Lucy S. Dawidowicz, *The War Against the Jews, 1933-1945* (New York: Holt, Rinehart and Winston, 1975).

6. For a survey of the "motivations and dynamics of antisemitism among Christian people," see A. Roy Eckart, *Christianity and the Children of Israel: A Theological Approach to the Jewish Question* (New York: King's Crown Press, 1948), chapter I; a briefer synopsis is found in Gregory Baum, *Is the New Testament Anti-Semitic?* (New York: Paulist Press, 1965), pp. 328-330, especially fn. 40.

trine.[7] Jesus' disputes with Jewish leaders, the caricature of Jewish ritual and synagogue, the "infidelity" of the formerly chosen —these and other anti-Judaistic themes run through the Holy Book of Christians. In recent years, numerous studies have looked carefully at the New Testament to glean from it whether, in fact, the very Scriptures are antisemitic.[8] These investigations come to different conclusions, but at least it can be said, "Christianity [especially the New Testament] wrongly understood offers a constant temptation for hostility against the Jews and the Synagogue."[9] In an effort to point out the polemical and apologetic character of the Scriptures, some exegetes claim that the New Testament writings need careful explanation so that they not be misunderstood,[10] while others suggest that

7. This view is supported by the results of the famous study of Charles Glock and Rodney Stark, *Christian Beliefs and Anti-Semitism* (New York: Harper and Row, 1966).

8. E.g., Markus Barth, "Was Paul an Anti-Semite?" *JES* 5 (1968):78-104; Gregory Baum, *Is the New Testament Anti-Semitic?*; Dominic M. Crossan, "Anti-Semitism and the Gospel," *Theological Studies* 26 (1965):189-214; Joseph Fitzmyer, "Anti-Semitism and the Cry of 'All the People,' " *Theological Studies* 26 (1965):667-671; Gerald O'Collins, "Anti-Semitism in the Gospel," *Theological Studies* 26 (1965):663-666; Rosemary Ruether, "Theological Anti-Semitism in the New Testament," *The Christian Century* 85 (1968):191-196; *idem, Faith and Fratricide*, pp. 64-116.

9. Gregory Baum, *Is the New Testament Anti-Semitic?* p. 329; this book, written in the late 1950's, was revised in 1965. In his recent "Introduction" to Rosemary Ruether's *Faith and Fratricide*, Baum has changed his position. At the time of writing the first volume, Baum "was still convinced that the anti-Jewish trends in Christianity were peripheral and accidental, not grounded in the New Testament itself but due to later developments, and that it would consequently be fairly easy to purify the preaching of the Church anti-Jewish bias" (p. 3, *Faith and Fratricide*). He then states that the book he wrote in the late 1950's "no longer represents my position on the relationship between Church and Synagogue." (p. 4, *ibid.*). It is difficult, in light of these two statements, to know whether he would answer the question posed by his first book in the affirmative now, or whether he would merely (perhaps this is more than enough) affirm that "anti-Jewish trends" had their root in the New Testament —which is another matter.

10. Bruce Vawter, "Are the Gospels Anti-Semitic?" *JES* 5 (1968):473-487, esp. p. 477; Kurt Schubert, "The People of the Covenant," in *Brothers in Hope*, pp. 132-158, edited by John M. Oesterreicher (New York: Herder and Herder, 1970), esp. pp. 143-157.

the Scriptures be expurgated of anti-Judaic expressions and affirmations.[11]

Whether the New Testament is antisemitic or not, there is
no dispute that it was read in an antisemitic way by some in the
Church, especially by some of the early Fathers.[12] Even as recently as this century, some Church leaders could still say:

> After the death of Christ Israel was dismissed from the ser-
> vice of Revelation. She did not know the time of her visita-
> tion. She had repudiated and rejected the Lord's Anointed,
> had driven Him to the Cross . . . . The Daughters of Sion
> received the bill of divorce and from that time forth As-
> suerus wanders, forever restless, over the face of the
> earth.[13]

Besides the holocaust and recent study of the theological
basis for antisemitism, another historical datum has forced
Christians to reflect on the meaning of Judaism's survival and
validity—the emergence of the state of Israel. Many Christians,
victims (and perpetrators) of the myth that the Jewish people
were accursed to wander the earth until the Second Coming and
were, at best, an anachronism after 70 C.E., have had to re-
evaluate their position in the light of the Jews' returning to their
original homeland. In short, traditional Christian beliefs about
salvation history and the Jewish people are called into question

11. E.g., Blu Greenberg, "Report of a Jewish Teacher," *The Ecumenist* 12
(1974):84-86. The special commission for the implementation of the directives of
Vatican II's "Declaration of the Church's Relation to Non-Christian Religions"
suggested in a 1969 "Working Document" that, in liturgical texts, "the phrase
'the Jews' in St. John can at times be translated, according to context, by 'the
leaders of the Jews' or the 'enemies of Jesus,' expressions that give a better rendering of the thought of the evangelist and avoid the appearance of involving the
Jewish people as such." Text from "Working Document," *Catholic Mind* 68
(1970):59-64 (p. 62).

12. See Alan T. Davies, *Anti-Semitism and the Christian Mind*, esp. pp.
53ff; Ben Zion Bokser, *Judaism and the Christian Predicament* (New York:
Alfred A. Knopf), 1967, pp. 207ff; Rosemary Ruether, *Faith and Fratricide*, pp.
117-182; James Parkes, *The Conflict of the Church and the Synagogue: A
Study in the Origins of Antisemitism* (London: The Soncino Press, 1934).

13. From a sermon of Cardinal Michael von Faulhaber, given in 1933,
quoted by Alan Davies, *Anti-Semitism*, p. 70.

by the undeniable fact of the resurgence of the state of Israel.[14]

Furthermore, new Christian interest in Rabbinic studies has provided a realization of the Jewish character of Jesus' teachings and the Jewish roots of the Christian faith.[15]

With such considerations—the meaning of Judaism's survival after Auschwitz, the emergence of the Jewish state, a new-found interest in Rabbinic studies—the stage was set for the landmark step forward of the Second Vatican Council's statement on the relationship of the Church to the Jewish people. A relationship of dialogue with the Jewish people was proposed, and this event spurred the Jewish and Christian communities to new hopes for improved relations. But the main condition for fruitful dialogue was not delineated in the Council's statement; it was only hinted at—a Christian repudiation of the super-sessionist theory:

The idea that with the coming of the church the historical mission of the Jewish people is fulfilled, that their role in sacred history was ended at that time and place, is the cornerstone of theological Antisemitism.[16]

The supersessionist theory[17] is variously expressed through

14. On this point, see Jacob Agus, "Israel and the Jewish-Christian Dialogue," *JES* 6 (1969):18-36; H. Berkhof, "Israel as a Theological Problem in the Christian Church," *JES* 6 (1969):329-347; Eva Fleischner, "The Religious Significance of Israel: A Christian Perspective," in *Jewish-Christian Relations*, pp. 17-25, edited by Robert Heyer (New York: Paulist Press, 1975); Rosemary Ruether, *Faith and Fratricide*, p. 228; Charlotte Klein, "The Theological Dimensions of the State of Israel," *JES* 10 (1973):700-715.

15. Eva Marie Fleischner, *Judaism in German Christian Theology Since 1945: Christianity and Israel Considered in Terms of Mission* (ATLA Monograph #8. Metuchen, NJ: The Scarecrow Press, Inc., 1975) p. 128f.

16. Franklin H. Littell, "Christendom, Holocaust," p. 490; cf. also his *The Crucifixion of the Jews*, p. 2.

17. William H. Harter, "A Methodology for the Analysis of Texts used in 'Displacement Theologies'" (unpublished paper, New York: Lutheran World Federation, 1974), has isolated texts from the Gospel open to displacement interpretations. He has arranged them into the following categories: "1) synonymous role for Church and Synagogue; 2) Church as fulfillment of Jewish hopes; 3) conflict with Judaism; 4) allocation of guilt or responsibility; 5) inclusion of Gentiles, Church as the light to the Gentiles; 6) displacement."

the history of Christianity: the Church as the "new (and there-fore, better) Israel," the Church as the new chosen people, Christ as the absolute fulfillment of the Old Testament,[18] the Is-raelite people as the (mere) preparation for the Christian faith,[19] the new covenant supplanting the old.[20] Against such a univocal reading of the Hebrew Scriptures, Roman Catholic exegete Ro-land E. Murphy has written:

> Rather the Old Testament must be understood on its own terms before its relationship to the New Testament can be properly appreciated. . . . Catholic theological exegesis has much to learn from the Jewish understanding of it [the Hebrew Scriptures].[21]

The cumulative effect of some or all of these superses-sionist expressions is that, while Israel was the beloved of God at one time, after she missed her visitation, she lost her election, and thus her right to existence—she is a cursed nation or, at best, an anachronistic one. In a persuasive article on the notion of election, Lutheran scholar Nils A. Dahl points out:

18. Even the reference "Old Testament" as the name of the Hebrew Scrip-tures implies that it has been put out of date, made obsolete, by the New Tes-tament; hence the perennial Marcionite tendency of some in the Church.

19. E.g., "Christianity, so Christians believe, stands in relation to Judaism as the final event does to the preparatory, as the complete to the in-complete. . . . To us Christians, it [Judaism] is . . . a partial or unfulfilled religion whose completion is found in Christianity. . . . Thus, the Old Cove-nant wrought at Sinai finds its fulfillment in the New Covenant wrought by Christ in his death; the Old Israel its fulfillment in the New Israel, the church; the Old Law its fulfillment in the life and words of Jesus": W. D. Davies, "Christianity and Judaism," in *The Jewish Heritage Reader*, edited by Lily Edelman (New York: Taplinger Publishing Co., 1965), pp. 190f.

20. E.g., "Israel's reprobation serves to the election of the Gentiles. Cer-tainly Israel is not to blame for not having believed in God [sic]. . . . The sha-dow cast over Israel by God comes from God. It is the shadow of God himself, given solely as a mirror for those entered into the light, to make them realize the darkness from which they came [!]." Hans Urs von Balthasar, *Church and World* (New York: Herder and Herder, 1967), p. 170. For expression of the supersessionist idea from a prominent Catholic exegete, see Lucien Cerfaux, *The Church in the Theology of St. Paul* (New York: Herder, 1959), pp. 7-8.

21. Roland E. Murphy, "Present Biblical Scholarship as a Bond of Under-standing," in *Torah and Gospel: Jewish and Catholic Theology in Dialogue*, edited by Philip Scharper (New York: Sheed and Ward, 1966), pp. 89f.

The simplistic doctrine that Israel was rejected and the church chosen to be a new people of God is not really found within the New Testament, although it is adumbrated in some of the late writings.[22]

Rosemary Ruether, on the other hand, claims that this replacement theology is indeed found within the New Testament and early Christian teachings and that it was formulated as a result of the double Christian hermeneutic of spiritualizing the eschatological (John) and historicizing the eschatological (Luke); thus, the Church "won a historical existence for herself by negating and claiming to supersede the historical existence of Israel."[23]

Whether the supersessionist idea is found in the New Testament or after, it has no place in a Jewish-Christian dialogue, for this idea may lead the Christian to deny the Jewish participant (and, by extension, his people) the right to exist, to say nothing about whether his religion is a valid approach to God. Thus, many Christians, approaching Jews from a stance of dialogue, affirm the continuing validity of Judaism, not as a religious expression merely preliminary to full realization in Christianity, but as a viable, integrated, and fully adequate response to God's call for faithfulness as found in the Hebrew Scrip-

22. Nils A. Dahl, "Election and the People of God: Some Comments," in *Speaking of God Today: Jews and Lutherans in Dialogue*, edited by Paul Opsahl and Marc C. Tanenbaum (Philadelphia: Fortress Press, 1974), p. 36; for a counterview, cf. Kurt Hruby, "Peoplehood in Judaism and Christianity," *Theology Digest*, 22 (1974):3-12 (p. 11).

23. Rosemary Ruether, "Theological Anti-Semitism," p. 195.

24. E.g., Gregory Baum, "The Doctrinal Basis for Jewish-Christian Dialogue," *The Month* 224 (1967):233-235; A. Roy Eckardt, "End to the Christian-Jewish Dialogue," *Christian Century* 83 (1966):395; *idem*, "Toward an Authentic Jewish-Christian Relationship," *Journal of Church and State* 13 (1971):277; Joseph R. Estes, "Jewish-Christian Dialogue as Mission," *Review and Expositor* 68 (1971):9f; Charlotte Klein, "The Theological Dimensions," p. 710; Sr. Louis-Gabriel, "Christians, Jews, and Ecumenism," *Catholic Mind* 67 (1969):14; *et al.* Monika Hellwig finds scriptural foundation for a development of doctrine which would affirm the validity of the Jewish religion alongside Christianity; after surveying contemporary New Testament exegesis, Hellwig concludes that St. Paul gives "somewhat less than an unconditional validation of Judaism as a religion today from the Christian point of view. It would seem that Paul's teaching itself, however, does give the basis for such an unconditional validation" (from her "Proposal Towards a Theology of Israel as a Religious Community Contemporary with the Christian" [Ph.D. Dissertation, Washington: Catholic University of America, 1968], p. 154).

tures.[24] This position is based on the insight that, since the call has not been revoked, the response—the continued existence of the Jewish people—continues to be valid. This position does not claim that Israel's response is fully adequate in terms of the New Testament. Nevertheless, this affirmation carries with it many eschatological, soteriological, and Christological implications. Indeed, one theologian questions whether any dialogue is possible because of the specifically Christological implications of recognizing the validity of Judaism:

> The divergence between the Church and the Synagogue is fundamental and covers the whole sphere of human-Divine relationship. . . . In reality, there is no understanding between the two faiths: they possess no common denominator which could form the basis for a bridge theology . . . in their separateness their only legitimate relationship is that of continuous interrogation. . . . Between Church and Synagogue stands the Crucified. Church and Synagogue derive their existence from their attitude toward Him.[25]

Others, realizing the risk taken in such an affirmation, suggest a recasting of traditional eschatological, soteriological, ecclesiological, and Christological affirmations. They are scrupulous to excise any motive of "proselytism" from the dialogue and thus they ask themselves questions such as the following: If the Christian admits that the Jews are no longer the object of a "conversionist program," has the Christian thereby compromised the traditional Christian belief in the unique and sole mediation of Jesus Christ for salvation? From another perspective, if Judaism is admitted to be a continuing, valid religious expression, can one still say that Christ has fulfilled the messianic promise contained in the Hebrew Scriptures, especially when Judaism's continued existence is the very evidence that it does not believe Christ to be the Messiah? In a stance of dialogue,

25. Jakob Jocz, *The Jewish People and Jesus Christ: A Study in the Controversy Between Church and Synagogue* (London: SPCK, 1954 [revised from 1949]), pp. 263-264, quoted by permission. For a similar statement, cf. Melvin Tumin, *An Inventory and Appraisal of Research on American Anti-Semitism* (New York: Freedom Books, 1961).

can Christians continue to understand themselves as the New Chosen People, supplanting and replacing the original people to whom the promise was given? All these questions find a common point of departure in the one central issue, Christology. This observation has been made by more than a few Christian thinkers in their encounter with Judaism.[26] In short, can a Christian admit the continuing validity of Judaism without compromising his belief in the finality of Jesus Christ? Or, as A. Roy Eckardt has put the issue:

> Jesus of Nazareth, called the Christ, embodies the paradox of uniting Jews with Christians and of separating Jews from Christians. There is simply no way around this stern fact. Any discussion of the Jewish-Christian relationship must presuppose both elements in ultimate tension. . . . Is there a foundation for confessing at one and the same time that the Christ has come and yet that the divine choice of original Israel retains a positive, constructive effect?[27]

It seems to this writer that another affirmation (other than that of Judaism's validity), more epistemological than theological, forces the Christian in the Jewish-Christian dialogue to reevaluate his Christological claims—and that is the stance of dia-

---

26. E.g., Gregory Baum, "Theology after Auschwitz," p. 72; Jean Danielou, *The Jews, Views and Counterviews: A Dialogue* (New York: Paulist Press, 1967), p. 25; W. D. Davies, "Torah and Dogma: A Comment—," in *The Death of Dialogue and Beyond*, p. 139, edited by Sanford Seltzer and Max L. Stackhouse (New York: Friendship Press, 1969); Eva Marie Fleischner, Judaism," p. 126; Monika Hellwig, "Why We Still Can't Talk," in *Jewish-Christian Relations*, p. 27, edited by Robert Heyer (New York: Paulist Press, 1975); John T. Pawlikowski, "Christ and the Jewish Christian Dialogue: An Evaluation of Contemporary Perspectives" (Paper given at the American Academy of Religion, Washington, D.C., 26 October 1974); Rosemary Ruether, *Faith and Fratricide*, pp. 246ff; J. Coert Rylaardsdam. "Common Ground and Differences," *Journal of Religion* 43 (1963):261-270 (p. 267). For Jewish expressions of this same observation, cf. Eugene B. Borowitz. "Contemporary Christologies: A Jewish Response" (Paper given at the American Theological Society, April 1975); Hans Joachim Schoeps, *The Jewish-Christian Argument: A History of Theologies in Conflict* (London: Faber and Faber, 1963 [3rd ed]), p. 23.

27. A. Roy Eckardt, *Elder and Younger Brothers: The Encounter of Jews and Christians* (New York: Charles Scribner's Sons, 1967), p. 142. Quoted by permission.

logue itself.[28] If Jews are no longer the object of a conversa-
tionist program (as many Christians concede), if they are
partners in a dialogue, then the new dialogical relation between
the faiths presupposes some sort of equality where each has
something to contribute to the other, and, more telling, where
each lacks something which only the other can contribute. Some
Christians, to be sure, refrain from a conversionist stance vis-à-
vis the Jews only because the memory of Auschwitz is still all
too vivid.[29] But this position is not the one we are describing.
The very shift of assuming a dialogue relationship toward the
Jews, out of principle and not out of convenience, has Christological implications.[30] Further, I would contend that such Christological ramifications inherent in a dialogical posture have been
noted and pursued by a few scholars (indeed, it is presupposed
in Rosemary Ruether's book and John Pawlikowski's article;
see fn. 26). But there are also those who do not recognize the
Christological implications flowing from a dialogical stance,
and they may not see that such a radical Christological reformulation is needed. Nevertheless, these persons choose to describe their belief in Christ in certain ways in the encounter with

28. This has also been noted by Eva Fleischner, "Judaism," pp. 205ff.
Her study approaches the traditional Christian self-understanding as missionary
in a way similar to the way this study approaches Christology. Cf. also her
considerations of the characteristics of the Jewish-Christian dialogue, p. 142f.

29. E.g., see Fleischner, "The View of Judaism," pp. 140f. for a survey of
such thinkers.

30. Obviously, by "dialogue" we do not mean the situation where persons
gather out of curiosity to learn about the others' religious beliefs and practices.
Rather, dialogue here is meant to describe the situation where each party sin-
cerely believes that he has insight to share and something to learn, not only on a
phenomenological level, but in the very realm of faith, in the realm of coming
into contact with God. This issue has been carefully and realistically described
in Henry Siegman's essay, "Dialogue with Christians: A Jewish Dilemma,"
Judaism 20 (1971) 93-103; cf. also Martin Buber, *Two Types of Faith* (London:
Routledge and Kegan Paul, Ltd., 1951), p. 174; Christopher Hollis, "Catholic-
Jewish Dialogue" (Paper presented at the International Conference of Christians and Jews, York University, Toronto, September 2-6, 1968): Dialogue is
not a mere technique of communication but a "principle of the way in which
one regards the other" (p. 3); but see Joseph R. Estes, "Jewish-Christian Dialogue as Mission," pp. 5-16.

Judaism and tend to ignore other formulations.[31] This is neither intellectually dishonest nor religiously unfaithful, for the Christian faith has always expressed itself in dialogue with (and therefore been influenced by) the cultures and thought patterns it has come in contact with—witness the influence of Aristotelian and other Greek philosophies on traditional Christological formulae. Indeed, when anyone enters into dialogue with another—business arbitration, philosophical debate, political negotiations—he is careful about his use of language, first, in order not to offend the other, and, second, in order to put forth accurately his position. However, in pursuing the first, the second is necessarily changed in the process. More specifically, some, inspired by a Mannheimian critique of ideological use of language by dominant groups,[32] suggest that the effort to make "theological room" for Israel means consciously to change one's position.[33]

31. On this very point, Gregory Baum's observation is worthy of consideration: "If the Church completes its christological and ecclesiological teaching without reflecting on its relation to Israel, and only afterward, when its basic teaching is defined, introduces the acknowledgement that the Jews remain God's chosen people and that therefore their religion has an abiding significance before God, this late recognition can no longer be integrated into the central Christian doctrines: it will remain marginal and ineffectual." "Introduction," p. 6. Quoted by permission.

32. See Karl Mannheim, *Ideology and Utopia: An Introduction to the Sociology of Knowledge* (New York: Harcourt, Brace and World, Inc., 1936), chapter II.

33. An interesting way of considering this sensitivity to ideological misuse of language and doctrine is that this sensitivity makes the avoidance of potentially anti-Judaic doctrines (with their not-inevitable expression in antisemitism) the hermeneutical principle for Christian self-understanding. For some, the pursuit of truth may dictate striving first for adequate doctrinal formulation, which striving is "uncluttered" by concerns of moral ramifications or ideological misuse; only afterwards do they consider accommodations where there is possible misuse of these formulated doctrines. This might be (simplistically) categorized into the opposition between voluntaristic/moralistic versus intellectualist orientations. The former accuses the latter of insensitivity to moral/ideological ramifications of doctrinal statements; the latter accuses the former of moralism, indifference to the question of truth, and of being unaware that right doctrine necessarily spills over into right action. Obviously, this dilemma will not be solved here; indeed, perhaps the dilemma is only an expression of the ongoing dialectical relationship between theory and praxis. But at least one way of understanding the Jewish-Christian dialogue, sensitive to the temptation of antisemitism in Christian theology, is the effort of bringing doctrinal understanding and ethical theory into harmony.

Thus a host of factors have contributed to bringing Christians and Jews into a relation of dialogue—the horrors of Auschwitz, the rise of the Israeli state, interest in Rabbinic studies, Christian reflection on its history of theological anti-Judaism, and Christian recognition of the continuing religious validity of Judaism. These factors, combined with the stance of dialogue itself, have thrown Christian thinkers into a careful re-evaluation of traditional Christological affirmations and expressions, or have dictated which Christological affirmations will be emphasized in the Christian-Jewish encounter.

It is the intention of this thesis, then, to survey the thought and expression of Christians in their official statements about, and informal dialogue with, the Jewish people in order to trace whatever Christologies—whether explicit or implicit—may be discernible. We will describe, compare, and contrast the Christological affirmations made by Christians in the current Christian-Jewish dialogue (primarily since Vatican II), and we will conclude with a few questions and suggested directions for further development, especially highlighting implications for the Christian mission and for the Christian dialogue with non-Jewish world religions.

II
A Survey of Formal
Church Statements
on the Relation of
Judaism and Christianity

A.

VATICAN II

Perhaps the most significant religious event in the twentieth century was the Second Vatican Council. In response to the modern world, part of which includes the Christian Church's failure with regard to Auschwitz, the Roman Catholic Church addressed itself to concerns, some of which were in relation to Judaism, both of the past and of the present. Not only was the Council a response to these areas of common concern, but the responses themselves laid the groundwork for a dialogic relationship with the Jewish people. Although it would be asking too much of the Council documents that they reflect a matured and fully thought-out blueprint of the Church's relation to the Synagogue, nevertheless the documents do provide new directions which only subsequent dialogue could exploit, develop, and enlarge upon. Indeed, the very fact that the documents opened up possibilities for solutions, rather than providing solutions, is instructive.

For our purposes, then, we will look to those parts of the Council decrees which speak of the Jewish people. It is important to note from the beginning, however, that, with the exceptions of the "Declaration on Religious Freedom" and the "Pastoral Constitution of the Church in the Modern World," the

Council documents are addressed to members of Catholic Christianity for their own self-understanding. Thus, with regard to our subject—Jewish-Christian relations—the claim can be only very modest. The documents are not addressed to the Jewish people, but rather they are an exhortation to Catholic Christians to expand their own self-understanding in recognizing the Church's debt to the people of Israel. But this is to get ahead of ourselves.

A second principle to keep in mind is that these documents —although overwhelmingly approved by the one and same body of men—were nevertheless written by different groups. Therefore the viewpoint and concerns are different from document to document. It is for this reason that we will look at the following documents individually ("Dogmatic Constitution on the Church," "Dogmatic Constitution on Divine Revelation," "Pastoral Constitution on the Church in the Modern World," and "Declaration on the Relation of the Church to Non-Christian Religions"), followed by a brief survey of appropriate documents which do not mention Israel ("Decree on Ecumenism" and the "Decree on the Church's Missionary Activity"), and then we will offer a synthetic appraisal of the Christologies at work in these documents.

1. *"Dogmatic Constitution on the Church"*

First in importance of the Council documents (although not the central document for our purpose) is the "Dogmatic Constitution on the Church." Here the Council Fathers enunciated the value and necessity of understanding the Church as the new people of God. In primarily two places, there are extended references to the relationship of the Church to Israel.

The first such reference is article 9:

It has pleased God, however, to make men holy and save them not merely as individuals without any mutual bonds but by making them into a single people, a people which acknowledge Him in truth and serve Him in holiness. He therefore chose the race of Israel as a people unto Himself. With it He set up a covenant. Step by step He taught this people by manifesting in its history both Himself and the decree of His will, and by making it holy unto Himself. All these things, however, were done by way of preparation and as a figure of that new and perfect covenant which was to be ratified in Christ, and of that more luminous revelation which was to be given through God's very Word made flesh. . . . Christ instituted this new covenant, that is to say, the new testament, in His blood (cf. 1 Cor. 11:25), by calling together people made up of Jew and Gentile, making them one, not according to the flesh but in the Spirit.

This was to be the new People of God. For those who believe in Christ, who are reborn not from a perishable but from an imperishable seed through the Word of the living God . . . that messianic people has for its head Christ. . . .

Israel according to the flesh, which wandered as an exile in the desert, was already called the Church of God. . . . Likewise the new Israel which, while going forward in this present world, goes in search of a future and abiding city . . . is also called the Church of Christ. . . . For He has bought it for Himself with His blood . . . has filled it with His Spirit, and provided it with those means which befit it as a visible and social unity. God has gathered together as one all those who in faith look upon Jesus as the author of salvation and the source of unity and peace, and has established them as the Church, that for each and all she may be the visible sacrament of this saving unity.[1]

1. "Dogmatic Constitution on the Church," Article 9, in *The Documents of Vatican II*, pp. 25f, edited by Walter M. Abbott (New York: Herder and Herder/Association Press, 1966) [hereafter, "Abbott"]. Quoted by permission.

Quite apparent in these few paragraphs is the basis for, if not the expression of, a supersessionist doctrine. The document mentions that Israel's covenanted relation with God was "done by way of preparation and as a figure of that new and perfect covenant which was to be ratified in Christ, and of that more luminous revelation which was to be given through God's very Word made flesh." Certainly the Christological claims made in this section are quite absolute, although a case could be made that Christ assumed a role of a new Moses in calling together a larger, more inclusive people. While use of "old" and "new" designations abound,[2] there is no reference to God repudiating his first people; indeed, the document calls the first people the Church of God and the second, the Church of Christ. Those who believe in Christ gather around him as the "author of salvation"; nothing, however, is said about the fate or validity of the original people of God. The Christology here is less "Christ as fulfiller of the prophecies" than it is "Christ the founder of the new people of God—Christ as the new Moses."[3]

Other assertions of the absolute, universal necessity of the "one people of God" (cf. article 13), open to less flexible interpretations, are to be found; however, they are not in the context of statements about the relation of the Church to Israel.

The second major reference to the relation between the Church and Israel is found in articles 16-17. Here the document gives a pre-eminent, privileged place to Israel:

Finally, those who have not yet received the gospel are related in various ways to the People of God. In the first place there is the people to whom the covenants and the promises were given and from whom Christ was born ac-

2. H. Berkhof, "Israel as a Theological Problem," p. 335, with reference to the designation "the New Israel," observes that "the name Israel is never used in the New Testament for another, more spiritualized community apart from Israel, called the Church", on "New Israel," cf. also Alan T. Davies, "The Jews in an Ecumenical Context: A Critique," *JES* 5 (1968):488-506, p. 493; Cornelius Rijk, "Some Observations on a Christian Theology of Judaism," *Service International de Documentation Judéo-Chrétienne* [hereafter, *SIDIC*] 5 (1972:#1):3-7, p. 11.

3. Cf. Aloys Grillmeier, "Commentary," pp. 155f, on this point, in *Commentary on the Documents of Vatican II*, vol. I, edited by Herbert Vorgrimler (New York: Herder and Herder, 1967) [hereafter, "Vorgrimler"].

cording to the flesh (cf. Rom. 9:4-5). On account of their fathers, this people remains most dear to God, for God does not repent of the gifts He makes nor of the calls He issues (cf. Rom. 11:28-29).[4]

Here the Council affirms that Israel "remains most dear to God"[5] and that it was from Israel that Jesus was born. Here Jesus is seen as the link of relationship, rather than the stumbling block, between Christianity and Judaism. Nevertheless, this section ends with the hope and intention of bringing all peoples into "the People of God, the Body of the Lord."[6]

2. *"Dogmatic Constitution on Divine Revelation"*

The "Dogmatic Constitution on Divine Revelation"—like all Council documents, the product of numerous compromises —speaks about the revelation of God to his people, first in the Hebrew Scriptures and then in the New Testament. Although the document does not treat of the validity of Judaism today or of its relation to Christianity, it does make some Christological assertions in contexts which describe the relationship between God's revelation in the Hebrew and Christian Scriptures. For example:

Then, at the time He had appointed, He called Abraham in

4. "Constitution on the Church," Art, 16, Abbott, p. 34. Quoted by permission. Markus Barth, "Salvation from the Jews," *JES* 1 (1964):323-326, expressed keen disappointment that the schema on the Jews was not included in the document on the Church, especially in light of Romans 9-11 and Ephesians 2.

5. Some commentators have been rightfully offended that the enduring relationship between God and the Jewish people is founded only on the faithfulness of ancestors', rather than on Judaism's contemporary, faithfulness to God. Cf. A. Roy Eckardt, *Elder Brother*, p. 115, fn. 32; Rabbi Siegman, quoted in *The Dialogue* #34 (1966), p. 4: "Surely there must be some basis for divine love for Israel in addition to the saving intervention of the pre-Christian patriarchs."

6. Grillmeier's commentary (fn. 3 of this chapter) says more than the Constitution in affirming that Christ fulfilled Israel's promise "in such a new way . . . that a believing Israel would have been the new people of God. The Church has taken up the heritage of Israel, but it is still offered to the people which was first called" (p. 182).

order to make of him a great nation (cf. Gen. 12:2). Through the patriarchs, and after them through Moses and the prophets, He taught this nation to acknowledge Himself as the one living and true God, provident Father and just Judge, and to wait for the Savior promised by Him. In this manner He prepared the way for the gospel down through the centuries. . . .

The Christian dispensation, therefore, as the new and definitive covenant, will never pass away, and we now await no further new public revelation before the glorious manifestation of our Lord Jesus Christ.[7]

These words, at the beginning of the Council decree, place the tenor of the whole document in a decidedly Christological context—not only both testaments have their end in Christ but all revelation history as well. Nevertheless the Christological focus does not express fulfillment in the Christ of the past, but only anticipates complete fulfillment in the future. Thus it is interesting to note how the final draft, by its *eschatological* focus,

. . . shows from within [Christian] faith the provisional nature of Christianity and hence its relatedness to the future which exists together with the connection with the Christ event that has taken place once and for all, so that it is impossible to state the one [Christological] without the other [eschatological].[8]

7. "Dogmatic Constitution on Divine Revelation," Arts. 3, 4, Abbott, pp. 112f; in discussions on messianism in the Hebrew Scriptures, there is the often repeated observation that Judaism looked more to a messianic age than to a personal messiah. E.g., cf. John T. Pawlikowski, "Issues in Catholic-Jewish Dialogue," *SIDIC* 7 (1974):#2:22-28, p. 27; F. C. Grant, *Ancient Judaism and the New Testament* (New York: The Macmillan Co., 1959), p. 22; Hans Joachim Schoeps, *The Jewish Christian Argument*, p. 26; Ellis Rivkin, "The Meaning of Messiah in Jewish Thought," *Union Seminary Quarterly Review* 26 (1972):383-406 (p. 384); Rosemary Ruether, "Theological Anti-Semitism," p. 193; James Parkes, *Prelude to Dialogue: Jewish-Christian Relationships* (New York: Schocken Books, 1969), p. 55; W. P. Eckert, "Messianism and the Church," *Encounter Today* 4 (1969):21-29 (p. 29).

8. Joseph Ratzinger, "Commentary on the Dogmatic Constitution on Divine Revelation," in Vorgrimler, 3:177.

Later, in the section of the Constitution devoted to the Old Testament, the Council Fathers declared:

In carefully planning and preparing the salvation of the whole human race, the God of supreme love, by a special dispensation, chose for Himself a people to whom He might entrust His promises. First He entered into a covenant with Abraham . . . and, through Moses, with the people of Israel. . . . To this people which He had acquired for Himself, He so manifested Himself through words and deeds as the one true and living God that Israel came to know by experience the ways of God with men, and with God Himself speaking to them through the mouth of the prophets, Israel daily gained a deeper and clearer understanding of His ways and made them more widely known among the nations. . . . The plan of salvation, foretold by the sacred authors, recounted and explained by them, is found as the true word of God in the books of the Old Testament: these books, therefore, written under divine inspiration, remain permanently valuable.

The principal purpose to which the plan of the Old Covenant was directed was to prepare for the coming both of Christ, the universal Redeemer, and of the messianic kingdom, to announce this coming by prophecy . . . and to indicate its meaning through various types. . . . These same books, then, give expression to a lively sense of God, sound wisdom about human life, and a wonderful treasury of prayers, and in them the mystery of our salvation is present in a hidden way. Christians should receive them with reverence.

God, the inspirer and author of both testaments, wisely arranged that the New Testament be hidden in the Old and the Old be made manifest in the New. For, though Christ established the New Covenant in His blood, still the books of the Old Testament with all their parts, caught up into the proclamation of the Gospel, acquire and show forth their full meaning in the New Testament . . . and in turn shed light on it and explain it.[9]

Chapter IV, just quoted, sought to express that "salvation is a preparation for the fulfillment of the ways of God in Jesus Christ, who is the 'end of the Law' (Rom. 10:4); as the Word of God, however, the Old Testament retains its permanent importance."[10]

Again the Council affirms the Old Testament as the Word of God which "remains permanently valuable" in itself and in order to understand the New Testament. One might argue whether the Christian Church has legitimately used the Old Testament to describe its belief in Christ as Messiah, especially with regard to prophecy/fulfillment and the taking over of Old Testament texts to describe Jewish "unbelief" after Christ. On the other hand, the document strongly affirms the anti-Marcionite doctrine of the Church, so much so that Christ is said to be incomprehensible without the enlightening guide of the Old Testament. This sort of exegesis of the preparatory character of the Old Testament has grave implications for Christian attitudes toward those who believe it to be a misinterpretation, for those who do not see the same Christological hermeneutic active in it. But one can only speculate on the devastating effects that might have befallen God's chosen people if the Church had not continually reaffirmed its anti-Marcionite doctrine, or, more telling, if it had not affirmed that position in the first place.[11] Also it is important to note again that this document is addressed to Christians for whom such a minimalist affirmation may nevertheless be absolutely crucial.

9. "Divine Revelation," Arts. 14-16, Abbott, pp. 121f. Quoted by permission.

10. Beda Rigaux, "Commentary," Vorgrimler, 3:247. Used by Permission of the Seabury Press, Inc.

11. As Jewish scholar Michael Wyschogrod has observed: "We must be grateful that, Marcion and Harnack notwithstanding, and in spite of this erroneous reading of Paul [Paul's speaking of Torah to Gentiles as if it were his full evaluation of Torah, equally applicable to Jew and Gentile] the Church clung to the Hebrew Bible. And because it did, dialogue between Christians and Jews is possible." In "The Law: Jews and Gentiles," p. 14, in *Speaking of God Today*, edited by Paul Opsahl. Quoted by Permission.

Another opening for development of the independent validity of the Hebrew Scriptures (although not providing that development itself) is the first phase of article 15: "The principal purpose"—but not the only purpose—of the Old Testament is preparation for Christ. It is interesting that the "Working Document on Jewish-Christian Relations," inadvertently released by Cardinal Lawrence Shehan in 1969, picks up on this opening and develops it:

> The Old Testament should not be understood exclusively in reference to the New, nor reduced to an allegorical significance, as is so often done in the Christian liturgy.[12]

There is no doubt, however, that the overwhelming hermeneutical principle at work in this Vatican II Document with regard to the Old Testament is to see it primarily as a preparation for the Christian belief in Christ as the fulfillment of prophecy and the finality of revelation. Openings for development appear, however; and perhaps foundations are to be found for a resolution to understanding the relationship between Judaism and Christianity—as a dispute over interpretation of the commonly-held Hebrew Scriptures, with Jesus the Christ as the hermeneutical principle for the Christian understanding of these books.[13]

3. *"Pastoral Constitution on the Church in the Modern World"*

The longest of the Council documents, the "Pastoral Constitution on the Church in the Modern World," contains only

12. "Working Document on Jewish-Christian Relations," *Catholic Mind* 68 (1970):59-64; but see the "Guidelines and Suggestions for Implementing the Conciliar Declaration '*Nostra Aetate*,'" Commision for Religious Relations with Jews, 1975, in *Jewish-Christian Relations*, pp. 76-82 (New York: Paulist Press, 1975), edited by Robert Heyer, especially "II. Liturgy."

13. Cf. W. D. Davies, "Torah and Dogma," pp. 134ff; Roland E. Murphy, "Present Biblical," pp. 89f; Jacob Petuchowski "Introduction" to John M. Oesterreicher, *The Rediscovery of Judaism: A Re-Examination of the Conciliar Statement on the Jews*, p. 13 (South Orange, N.J.: Institute of Judaeo-Christian Studies, 1971) for examples of those who understand the division between Christianity and Judaism as primarily a difference in interpreting the Hebrew Scriptures.

one reference to the Jewish people, and this only as an example of how God calls men in social units as well as individually:

> So from the beginning of salvation history He has chosen men not just as individuals but as members of a certain community. Revealing His mind to them, God called these chosen ones 'His people' (Ex. 3:7-12), and, furthermore, made a covenant with them on Sinai.

> This communitarian character is developed and consummated in the work of Jesus Christ. For the very Word made flesh willed to share in the human fellowship.[14]

Although it would be laying too much of a theological burden on this one passage to make it a focus of reflection, it is interesting to speculate that one could conclude that God does not cease to call people as a social unity—the Jewish people—and the continued function of the Jewish people is to witness to this very truth. Christianity witnesses to, and forms its missionary theology upon, the fact that God calls people individually as well. The two-covenant theory, first described by Franz Rosenzweig, is a logical outcome of this sort of thinking. Nevertheless, the Christology expressed in this context is fulfillment Christology—Christ "develops and consummates the communitarian nature of salvation." While evidence for this conclusion in the gospels is forced, the Pastoral Constitution is not a theological treatise—it is a pastoral document describing and proposing Church life.

4. *"Declaration on the Relation of the Church to Non-Christian Religions"*

The fate and history of the "Declaration on the Relation of the Church to Non-Christian Religions" was as rocky and em-

---

14. "Pastoral Constitution on the Church in the Modern World," Art. 32, Abbott, p. 230. Quoted by permission.

battled as any schema at the Council.[15] First a part of the "Dogmatic Constitution on the Church," then in the "Decree on Ecumenism,"[16] and almost in the "Declaration on Religious Freedom," the Council's statement on the Jewish people became part of the Declaration which considered the relation of the Church to various world religions. Even this position among the so-called pagan religions disappointed many who saw this placement as a denial of Judaism's special relationship to Christianity. The history of these kinds of shifts and political maneuvers is interesting and significant, but our concern here is only with the final version, with particular attention to the Christology expressed therein.

There is no doubt that the final version of the Declaration approved by the Council Fathers had been "watered down," but the complex constellation of reasons for this deserves more attention than it has received.[17]

Article 4 of the Declaration is concerned with the Church's relation to Judaism, and it begins with the positive observation that Abraham is the common father of Jews and Christians. Following the distinction between the Church of God and the Church of Christ (cf. p. 21), the Declaration asserts that those who follow Christ must look for their beginnings in the Jewish election. The Church continues (present tense) to draw sustenance from the "root of that good olive tree" and Christ should

15. For the most complete history of the document, see John M. Oesterreicher, "Commentary," in Vorgrimler, 3:1-136, especially pp. 51-53 for the debate whether the statement on the Jews should be included in the "Decree on Ecumenism."

16. For the text of the statement on the Jews while it was still part of the appendix to the "Decree on Ecumenism," see "De Judaeis," *The Tablet* 218 (1964):1093f.

17. Thus the rather hasty description of the document as an "abortion" by A. Roy Eckardt, *Your People, My People: The Meeting of Jews and Christians* (New York: Quadrangle Books, 1974), p. 74; besides Oesterreicher's article cited above, for a history of the text, see Rene Laurentin, *Commentary on the Declaration on the Relation of the Church to Non-Christian Religions* (Ramsey, N.J.: Paulist Press, 1966), pp. 17-47. For a sympathetic rendering of the history of the text, see Augustin Cardinal Bea, *The Church and the Jewish People* (London: Geoffrey Chapman, 1966). It is interesting to note in Bea's apology for the conciliar statement the frequent reference to Israel's role as preparation for Christianity; cf. pp. 99ff, 120f, 126, 128.

be a cause of unity rather than of division (paragraph 3).[18] Not only supernatural but natural roots for Christianity are found in the Jewish people, for Jesus sprang from the Jewish people (paragraph 4).

If a foundation for the continuing validity of Jewish faithfulness is present in the Declaration, it is to be found in the fifth paragraph where the Council Fathers declared that "the Jews still remain most dear to God," although, as some have pointed out before (cf. p. 17, fn. 5), the qualification "because of their fathers" is unfortunate.[19] Interestingly, the Declaration uses the word "Lord" where it could have specifically referred to Christ when it speaks of the eschatological resolution, when "all peoples will address the Lord in a single voice." Paragraph six, short but significant, commits the Church to a posture of brotherly dialogue vis-à-vis the Jewish people.

Paragraph seven speaks of the historical facts surrounding the crucifixion (notably that only a few Jewish leaders were responsible for Jesus' death, and that certainly any guilt for that action cannot be transferred to the Jews of today[20]) and makes the theological conclusion that "although the Church is the new people of God, the Jews should not be presented as repudiated or cursed by God, as if such views followed from the Holy Scriptures." The Council apparently did not see the possible contradiction here—it is difficult to claim that the Jews are not repudiated in *some* way if the Christian Church is *the* new peo-

18. On this point, John Sheerin (*The Dialogue* #34 [1966]:6) comments: "Many Jews feel that the Jewish statement shows respect for the prophets and the religion of ancient Israel but not for the religion of modern Jews. If this were true, the Council would be saying in effect that the only good Jews are dead Jews. This was certainly not the mind of the Council." Quoted by permission.

19. On this point, cf. Cornelius A. Rijk, "Catholics and Jews after 1967— A New Situation" *New Blackfriars* 50 (1968):15-26 (p. 20); John M. Oesterreicher, *The Rediscovery*, p. 24: "True, the Council did not expressly say that Judaism is a living faith and a grace-filled way of life. But, let me ask, does a lover ever preface his profession of love by stating his philosophical conviction that his beloved is real, not a figment of his imagination? This is very much the way it is with the statement." Quoted by permission.

20. On the issue of the Council's position on the charge of deicide, see Rene Laurentin, *Commentary*, pp. 30f, 65ff; John M. Oesterreicher, "Deicide as a Theological Problem," in *Brothers in Hope*, pp. 190-205; Jules Isaac, *The Teaching of Contempt*.

ple of God. The "theological room" opened up in previous paragraphs seems to be closed here.[21] However, the *reasoning* for the assertion that the Jewish people are neither repudiated nor accursed is significant—the Council does not take the tack that such a doctrine as "Israel accursed" should be avoided because it leads to persecutions and other unfortunate consequences. Rather these notions should be avoided because they are untrue.[22]

Finally, the section on the Church's relation to the Jewish people closes on a pair of Christological assertions. First, in response to the declaration that the crucifixion was not the result of Jewish conspiracy, the Council Fathers assert that Christ freely and lovingly embraced his death, which death was the result of all men's sins.[23] Secondly the Council asserts the absolute and universal efficacy of the cross of Christ. Although the Council in this document did not call on Christians to launch a conversionist program specifically toward the Jews, it reiterated "the duty of the Church's preaching to proclaim [*annuntiare*] the cross of Christ as the sign of God's all-embracing love and as the fountain from which every grace flows."[24]

5. *Other Documents and Conclusions*

The silence of the Council Fathers on the relation of the Church to Judaism in two other documents is significant, although it would be drawing too much from an argument from silence to exaggerate these omissions. The Council Fathers, in the statement on the Jews, committed the Church to a posture

21. But see Thomas F. Stransky, "Reflections," *The Dialogue* #34 (1966):8, who suggests that the assertion of Israel not being repudiated may be all the more forceful when put against the traditional belief in the Church's claim to be the people of God: "The 'although the Church is the new people of God' in no way closes discussion on the Jews being in some way also *of* the new people."

22. Cf. p. 11, fn. 33, for a more formal description of the distinction between these two kinds of argument.

23. This, of course, is not original with the Vatican II declaration; indeed, this sentiment informed the teaching of the *Catechism of the Council of Trent for Parish Priests*.

24. "Declaration on the Relation of the Church to Non-Christian Religions," Art. 4, Abbott, p. 667.

of dialogue with no mention about missions to the Jews. In the document on the missionary activity of the Church, however, the Fathers affirmed the traditional universal character of the Christian mission:

> The missionary activity [of the Church] finds its reasons in the will of God [quotation, 1 Tim. 2:4-5]. Therefore, all must be converted to Him as He is made known by the Church's preaching. All must be incorporated into Him by baptism, and into the Church which is His body. . . .

> Christ and the Church, which bears witness to Him by preaching the gospel, transcend every particularity of race or nation and therefore cannot be considered foreign any-where or to anybody.[25]

Whether the Church, in the midst of its effort to encourage a strong missionary movement, could have expressed itself with more qualification in regard to the Jewish people is doubtful.[26] For some, to have made an exception of the Jewish people in the Church's missionary program would have been tantamount to repudiating the commission of Christ to teach all nations and call into question the Church's belief in the sole mediatorship of Christ for salvation. It is significant that the Council Fathers referred to 1 Timothy 2:4-5 in its missionary justification, for there the New Testament writer asserts the sole mediatorship of Christ for salvation. A question raised by this thesis is whether one can formulate a Christology which does not compromise

25. "Decree on the Church's Missionary Activity," Arts. 7 and 8, Abbott, p. 593 "quoted by permission."

26. Gregory Baum's observation on the Council's diversity of views on mission is appropriate here (which observation illustrates the point that the documents were written by different groups): "Three separate documents dealt with the Church's mission. One of them, the 'Decree on Missionary Activity,' develops the traditional understanding of the missions as the evangelization of unbelievers. The 'Declaration on the Church's Relationship to Non-Christian Religions' regards mission as primarily creative dialogue with others, and the 'Constitution on the Church Today' looks upon the mission of the Church principally as her effort to enter into solidarity with the whole human race and to serve others so that life may become more human" (Baum, "The Doctrinal Basis," p. 241).

traditional Christological beliefs and yet, at the same time, admit the continuing validity (and therefore the continuing obligation of the Jews to be faithful to their call within Judaism) of the Jewish religion. At best, the Council documents are ambivalent on that question, perhaps even oblivious of it; nevertheless, the fact that the question stands in all its paradox and unresolvedness is a significant opening.

Many observers were quite disheartened that the Council did not include the statement on the Jews in its "Decree on Ecumenism." Perhaps the excitement generated by the possibility of new advances toward cooperation and unity with other Christian bodies made the Church neglect the fundamental division in the People of God.[27] Whatever the reason, in its decree the Council defined ecumenism as follows:

> Taking part in this movement, which is called ecumenical, are those who invoke the Triune God and confess Jesus as the Lord and Savior.[28]

To be sure, the Second Vatican Council opened some doors to further development,[29] but, read as a whole, the preponderant Christology expressed was one of fulfillment and absolute necessity for Christ as mediator of salvation. The Old Testament was most often understood as primarily (although not exclusively) preparatory to full consummation and flowering in Christianity, with Christ as the fulfillment of all Israel's hopes and prophecies.

Arthur Gilbert noted the Catholic Church's new directions with regard to the Jewish people, but he had certain questions about other movements. For instance, he denies

27. On this point, cf. John M. Oesterreicher's commentary in Vorgrimler, 3:51-53; Laurentin, "Commentary," *ad. loc.*; Bernard Leeming, *The Vatican Council and Christian Unity* (New York: Harper and Row, 1966), pp. 21f.

28. "Decree on Ecumenism," Abbott, Art. 1, p. 342; this formula follows closely that of the World Council of Churches.

29. Monika Hellwig, "Proposal," pp. 144-147, outlines eight significant points of progress in the conciliar documents with regard to the Jews: "The dogmatic development contained in the Second Vatican Council would seem to open the door far, far wider for further theological development of the Christian understanding of Israel than has taken place so far" (p. 147).

. . . that the purpose of Jewish history or the meaning of Jewish scripture is by way of 'preparation' for a more perfect or luminous Christianity that allegedly fulfills and completes the prophetic word. . . . Jews interpret the persistence of their particularity as an act of fidelity and a testimony of their love for God. [The Decree on Ecumenism] expresses Christian priority in such exclusive terms as to evoke inevitably a competitive and defensive Jewish retort.[30]

It should be remembered, however, that the documents of the Council were not drawn up *in dialogue with* the Jewish people, but sought rather to be expressions of Christian self-understanding done in the context of, and sensitivity to, the abiding reality of Judaism. The preliminary and cautious progress opens itself to, indeed invites, a clearer, more consistent resolution in subsequent, more focused, statements. Nevertheless, it is significant that bald statements of Christ's universal and absolute mediatorship are not found in the contexts of Jewish-Christian relationships, but are found in those areas where Israel is not mentioned. To be sure, in the contexts noted above where Israel is mentioned, Christ is seen as the fulfillment and answer to Israel's hopes, but Christ is also appealed to as the source of unity, rather than the cause of division, between Christianity and Judaism. This inconsistency, opened up by the Council, becomes the more conscious concern of subsequent Church declarations. It is now time to look at those subsequent Church statements on Jewish-Christian relations to see how they express Christology in the Jewish-Christian encounter.

---

30. From *"The Vatican Council and the Jews"* by Arthur Gilbert, (copyright 1968), permission of Harry N. Abrams, Inc., pp. 206, 209; Gilbert gives a particularly insightful history of the issues, especially from his viewpoint as a Jew, on pp. 67-196; cf. also the various drafts of the conciliar statement on the Jews, pp. 262-291. For other Jewish reaction to the statement on the Jews, cf. *The Dialogue* #34 (1966):3f.

B.
FORMAL STATEMENTS FROM CHRISTIAN CHURCHES
SINCE VATICAN II

1. *Roman Catholic Statements Since Vatican II*

Since Vatican II, various official organs of the Roman Catholic Church throughout the world have assessed the conciliar documents on the relation of the Church to Israel. They have tried to further theological reflection on the issues raised in the documents, and they have implemented practical applications of these reflections. The very fact that bishops' conferences (particularly in the United States) have addressed themselves to these concerns and have issued subsequent guidelines and inquiries indicates that the bishops understood the Council documents more as a beginning of reflection and reform than as a definitive blueprint or solution.

We will examine six of these documents, the latest of which was issued only in the last few months. While official documents are usually the last place one finds evidence of new departures in theological reflection, nevertheless scrutiny of these documents often yields insight into the drift of theological thinking which most probably will have an influence on the ordinary life of the Church.

a. *"Guidelines for Catholic-Jewish Relations"*[31]

Acknowledging that "in the United States lives the largest Jewish community in the world" (p. 11), the bishops' committee stated its intention to continue American leadership in fostering Jewish-Christian relations and cooperation. The statement, pri-

---

31. "In March, 1967, the Sub-Commission of Catholic Bishops in America, for Jewish Catholic affairs . . . published ten general principles and ten suggestions for programs by which Catholics can respond to the conciliar Document, *Nostra Aetate*": text reprinted in *SIDIC* 3 (1970): #2:10-13; for an interesting application of these guidelines on a diocesan level, see "New York, Rockville Centre, and Brooklyn: Guidelines for the Advancement of Catholic Jewish Relations," *SIDIC* 3 (1970):#2:16-21.

marily practical in nature, sought to implement in a practical way the main doctrinal thrusts of *Nostra Aetate*. Nevertheless, the statement strongly recommends certain themes for study and development; germane to our concern are the following:

d. A study of the life of Jesus and of the primitive Church in the setting of the religious, social and cultural features of Jewish life in the first century;

e. An explicit rejection of the historically inaccurate notion that Judaism of that time, especially that of Pharisaism, was a decadent formalism and hypocrisy, well exemplified by Jesus' enemies;

f. An acknowledgement by Catholic scholars of the living and complex reality of Judaism after Christ and the permanent election of Israel, alluded to by St. Paul (Rom. 9:29), and incorporation of the results into Catholic teaching.[32]

To be noted is the emphasis put upon the Jewishness of Jesus, which emphasis goes beyond the Council's general recommendation to remember the Jewish roots of Christianity. But more interesting than the attempt to correct attitudes resulting from inaccurate historical accounts (the concern of themes b, c, d, e, and g) is the statement's affirmation of the living reality of Judaism after Christ and the permanent election of Israel. Nowhere in the document is there a hint of, or foundation for, a supersessionist theology, although neither is there explicit repudiation of such a theology. One might counter that the incipient character of the statement precludes such supersessionist-tend-

32. *Ibid.*, pp. 12f. Mrs. Claire Huchet Bishop, long-time and respected authority on Jewish-Christian relations, made the following interesting comment on the Guidelines: "These excellent themes have a familiar ring to the ears of those of us who have been associated with Prof. Jules Isaac's work for the last twenty years. These very points were enumerated by him in his list of practical suggestions presented to John XXIII on June 13, 1960. Previously these same points had formed the basis for the Ten Seelisberg Points in 1947. And again, before that, they had been incorporated in Isaac's book *Jesus and Israel*, in 1946." Quoted in *The Dialogue*, #35 (June 1967):7. Quoted by permission.

ing doctrines—*or* one might say that the document indicates a sensitivity hitherto not present in Church or Council documents. In this statement—as well as in the ones which follow—there is hardly a well-worked-out Christology. Nevertheless it is instructive that the Christologies operative in them are not laden with fulfillment or absolutist claims. For the moment we can make this general statement about the Christologies operative in the documents; the positive Christological thrusts of the subsequent documents will be noted as we take each in turn.

The dynamic of dialogue persuades (not dishonestly) the use of certain language, and the process of dialogue may help Christians come to a new understanding of Christ when admitting "the living and complex reality of Judaism after Christ and the permanent election of Israel."

b. *"Working Document on Jewish-Christian Relations"*[33]

It should be noted from the start that this "Working Document" was not promulgated. We include it here to indicate directions which the Roman Catholic Church was taking in 1969. In itself, the document is quite remarkable for the progress it makes over the 1967 document. We quote from it extensively to illustrate some of these new and extended directions:

> Still too often Christians do not know what Jews are. They do not, in any case, see them as they are in themselves and they define themselves in their present and living reality, as the people of the Bible living in our midst. . . . This same God has revealed Himself to His people Israel and made to it the gift of the Torah. And He has confided to it a word that 'endures forever' (Is. 40:8), a word that has become an unquenchable source of life and prayer in a tradition that has not ceased to enrich itself through the centuries.

33. Prepared by a special commission for the implementation of the directives of Vatican II's "Declaration on the Relationship of the Church to Non-Christian Religions." The Document was made public in December 1969 by Cardinal Lawrence Shehan of Baltimore, a member of the Unity Secretariat. Text from *Catholic Mind* 68 (1970):59-64. Quoted by permission.

. . . reflection on the mystery of Israel is also indispensable for Christianity to define itself, both as to its origin and in its nature as People of God. Without question, many elements from diverse civilizations have ultimately contributed to making Christianity what it is in its doctrines and its institutions.

An effort must be made to understand better that the Old Testament retains its proper validity . . . this should not be denied by reason of the subsequent interpretation of the New Testament. The Old Testament should not be reduced to an allegorical significance, as is so often done in the Christian liturgy . . . the continuity of our faith with that of the Old Covenant should be underscored particularly from the point of view of the promises and the common expectation of their eschatological fulfillment.

Jesus, as also His disciples, was a Jew. He presented Himself as continuing and fulfilling the interior Revelation, the basic teachings of which He offered anew, using the same teaching methods as the rabbis of His time. The points on which He took issue with the Judaism of His time are fewer than those in which He found Himself in agreement with it. Whenever He opposed it, it was always from within the Jewish people, just as did the prophets before Him.

The history of Judaism does not end with the destruction of Jerusalem, but continues to develop in a rich spiritual tradition.

According to New Testament teaching, the Jewish people play an essential role in the eschatological fulfillment of history.[34]

---

34. *Ibid.*, pp. 60-63. According to an explanatory note in *SIDIC* 3 (1970):#2:22-24, this document was released "through an indiscretion." The results of efforts to issue a comprehensive set of guidelines did not come until December 1974, entitled, "Guidelines and Suggestions for Implementing the Conciliar Declaration, '*Nostra Aetate.*' " See below, section f.

Preliminary observations reveal the following points of progress:

—there is a call to let the Jews define themselves in their terms in the present;

—reflection on Israel affects the way the Church understands and defines itself; indeed, the encounter with Judaism will contribute to its doctrines [the very theme of this study];

—the Old Testament has meaning in and of itself, and not merely as a preparation for the New;

—not denying the fulfillment in Christ, the document speaks of the Old Testament prophecies and their *eschatological* fulfillment;

—there is emphasis on the Jewishness of Jesus, that Jesus was a faithful Jew and that when he challenged the religion of his times, he did not do so from the outside of that religion;

—to the Jewish people has been confided the enduring Word of God which has continued to be a source of life and prayer in the rich Jewish tradition.

Absent from this statement are any supersessionist notions; rather the statement comes close to expressing many tenets of the schism theory.[35] In affirming the "proper validity" of the Hebrew Scriptures the committee members refrained from Christologies which speak of absolute fulfillment in Christ, and from ecclesiologies which speak of the "new Israel," the "new People of God." Not denying that the Old Testament can be understood as preparation for the New, the document admits other interpretations as well. Interestingly the statement does not use "Christ" at all; references are to "Jesus" except once when the statement mentions that Christian unity is "willed by the Lord." Again, the Christology of the statement is neither conscious nor of lengthy consideration. But the emphases upon Jesus as a man, a Jewish man, part of a religious and cultural milieu, and, by implication, the fulfillment of the Old Testament only in the eschatological times—these are unmistakable.

35. On the schism theory, see Bernard Lambert, *Le Probleme oecumenique* (Paris: Centurion, 1962), II:ch. 11, pp. 597-656.

c. *"Noordwijkerhout: Pastoral Recommendations"*[36]

Very soon after the "Working Document" was released in the United States, the Dutch Church issued its longer and more detailed statement. Admitting that it went beyond the Conciliar statements, the Dutch Church asked forgiveness from the Jewish people for crimes done against them, condemned antisemitism, and called upon the Church in the Netherlands to study and appreciate its common patrimony with the Jewish people.

The passages which relate to our topic are the following:

> The Pastoral Council of the Roman Catholic Church in the Netherlands believes that, according to the Law, the Prophets and the Psalms, the Jewish people has been constituted for ever as a testimony of God's saving alliance with mankind. . . . God's promise *par excellence* to the Jewish people is the everlasting covenant. . . . The Pastoral Council believes that Jesus Christ, born under the Law, is the one whom the Prophets, the Righteous and Kings desired to see . . . because in Him the revelation of God's eternal love reached its plentitude. . . . The Pastoral Council states that in Jesus Christ, peace has been initiated, uniting the two worlds, and breaking down the wall of separation between Jews and Gentiles. . . . He shall come to complete this Peace. . . . That is why also the as yet unfulfilled promises of God to the Jewish people are held in honour in liturgical prayer.

> Any intention, or design, for proselytism must be rejected as contrary to human dignity and Christian conviction. Moreover, the position of the Jewish people with regard to the universal message of Christ cannot be equated with the position of those professing other non-Christian religions.

36. During the Plenary Session of the Pastoral Council of the Catholic Church in the Netherlands from 5 to 8 April, 1970, at Noordwijkerhout, a series of 'Pastoral Recommendations' were studied from a plan for 'Relations between Jews and Christians.' This final document was drawn up by the Sub-Commission 'The Church and Israel.' " Text from *SIDIC* 3 (1970):#2:25-32.

Belittling ideas about the Jewish people will inevitably live on as long as the preaching of Jesus and the apostles is detached from its historical Jewish background, and Christianity is presented as a system of abstract truths. The history of the Jewish people, before as well as after Christ, has to be considered in its particular meaning in Salvation History.

1. The Jewish people has to be considered as the people with whom God concluded his covenant for ever. The Old Testament does not exist only in function of the New Testament, but has its own significance in Jewish as well as in world history.

4. It is not self-evident at all that a complete rupture arose between Jews and Christians, since Jesus—born of a Jewish mother—never broke away from his attachment to his people. The young Church was rooted in the Jewish people.[37]

Points to be noted are:
—the Jewish people serves as an everlasting "testimony of God's saving alliance with mankind";
—Christ, the answer to prophetic hopes, did not fulfill all that the Jews expected; thus, the assertion of eschatological fulfillment;
—the Jews have a (yet undefined) relation to the message of Christ different from that of other non-Christian religions;
—Jewish history is crucial for understanding Jesus in his times and it is significant in the history of salvation after Jesus as well;
—the Old Testament has significance in itself and not only in function of the New Testament;
—Jesus never severed his relationship with Judaism.
Again, certain drifts may be detected in the Christology of this statement: partial fulfillment in Christ, ultimate fulfillment only in the end times; the Old Testament open to a non-Christological hermeneutic; Jesus can be understood only as

37. *Ibid.*, pp. 27-30.

standing faithfully within, and never repudiating, Judaism; the Jewish people's existence has abiding significance.

d. *"Christian-Jewish Relations at the
   Diocesan Synod of Vienna," October 23, 1970*[38]

Although this statement is much shorter than the preceding ones, the few points it makes with regard to our subject are worthwhile:

According to Rom. 9-11, the existence and history of Judaism are a mystery of salvation for Christians. Hence Christians should also interpret the existence of contemporary Judaism as part of the history of salvation. . . .

We firmly hold true, as stated by the Apostle Paul in Rom. 11 (see vvs. 1, 26, 28), that the new covenant in Christ has not nullified the promises of the Old Covenant. It is in the light of this text that all New Testament passages referring to Israel are also to be interpreted accordingly. We, Christians, may not regard the Jews as the People of God, once chosen, and later rejected.[39]

At the very least, the Christology at work here is one which does not abrogate the covenant made with Israel and which can co-exist with the abiding validity of Judaism.

e. *"Pastoral Orientation with Regard to the
   Attitudes of Christians Toward Judaism"*[40]

The French bishops call for a reappraisal of the Christian theology on Judaism based on the fact of present-day Judaism:

38. Text from *Encounter Today* 6 (1971):95-97.
39. *Ibid.*, p. 95.
40. Issued by the French Catholic Bishops, April 18, 1973; text from *Catholic Mind* 71 (Sept. 1973):51-57. Quoted by permission.

Even if, for the Christian, the covenant has been renewed in Jesus Christ, Judaism ought to be looked upon by Christians . . . primarily as a religious reality. One should not forget that by his obedience to the Torah and by his prayer, Jesus a Jewish man, through His mother the Virgin Mary, accomplished His ministry within the people of the covenant.

Israel and the Church are not complementary institutions. The permanence of the juxtaposition of Israel and the Church is the sign of the incompletion of God's design. The Jewish people and the Christian people are thus in a situation of mutual conflict, or, as St. Paul said, of 'jealousy' in regard to unity. . . . Jews and Christians are accomplishing their vocation by following distinct routes . . . jointly concerned for the Messianic Age.[41]

Familiar themes—Jesus in his Jewish milieu, Jesus as an obedient Jew, and ultimate eschatological fulfillment of Christian and Jewish messianic hopes—are found in the French Bishops' statement. This statement presents not so much a different position from other statements, but a reiteration of Christological themes common to other contemporary Church statements on Jewish-Christian relations.

f. *"Guidelines and Suggestions for Implementing the Conciliar Declaration 'Nostra Aetate' (No. 4)"*[42]

After apparently many revisions of the 1969 working document, the newly formed Vatican Commission for Religious Relations with Jews issued the official "Guidelines and Suggestions for Implementing the Conciliar Document *'Nostra Aetate'* (No. 4)." Among other things, the final draft omitted any mention of the state of Israel or of proselytizing in the dialogue. In

41. *Ibid.,* pp. 53, 54, 57. Quoted by permission.
42. Issued by the Roman Commission for Religious Relations with Jews, Cardinal Willebrands, president; text from *Jewish-Christian Relations,* pp. 76-81, edited by Robert Heyer (New York: Paulist Press, 1975).

fact, adding to the working document of 1969, the new Guidelines mention the necessity of the Church to preach Christ to all
nations:

> In virtue of her divine mission, and her very nature, the
> Church must preach Jesus Christ to the world. . . . [While
> respecting religious freedom], they [Christians] will strive
> to understand the difficulties which arise for the Jewish
> soul—rightly imbued with an extremely high, pure notion
> of the divine transcendence—when faced with the mystery
> of the incarnate Word.[43]

Rabbi Marc Tanenbaum of the American Jewish Committee regretted that the Commission felt compelled to insert this
missionary exigency into a document advocating dialogue. Such
a move "cannot but cast doubt on the motivation of the entire
dialogue."[44]

Seen in isolation, the new Guidelines appear to be a big
step forward, but, when compared with the working document,[45] the step forward is not quite so impressive. Indeed the
very issue with which we are concerned—Christology—has been
significantly recast from the working document. To illustrate,
we present the Christological sections of the Guidelines side-by-
side with those of the working document:

Working Document	*Guidelines*
An effort must be made to understand better that the Old Testament retains its proper validity. This should not be denied by reason of the subsequent interpretation of the New Testament. The Old Testament should not be understood exclusively in reference to the New, nor reduced to an al-	An effort will be made to acquire a better understanding of whatever in the Old Testament retains its own perpetual value . . . since that has not been cancelled by the later interpretation of the New Testament. Rather, the New Testament brings out the full meaning of the Old, while both Old

43. *Ibid.*, p. 77.
44. Quoted by John B. Sheerin, "Commentary," in *Jewish-Christian Relations*, p. 86, edited by Robert Heyer (New York: Paulist Press, 1975).
45. See section b above and fn. 33.

legorical significance, as is so often done in the Christian liturgy.

. . . the continuity of our faith with that of the Old Covenant should be underscored particularly from the point of view of the promises and the common expectation of their eschatological fulfillment.

Thus, the phrase 'the Jews' in St. John can at times be translated, according to context, by 'the leaders of the Jews' or the 'enemies of Jesus,' expressions that give a better rendering of the thoughts of the evangelist and avoid the appearance of involving the Jewish people as such.

Jesus, as also His disciples, was a Jew. He presented Himself as continuing and fulfilling the interior Revelation, the basic teachings of which he offered anew. The points on which He took issue with the Judaism of His time are fewer than those in

and New illumine and explain each other. This is all the more important since liturgical reform is now bringing the text of the Old Testament ever more frequently to the attention of Christians.

. . . emphasis will be laid on the continuity of our faith with that of the earlier Covenant, in the perspective of the promises, without minimizing those elements of Christianity which are original. We believe that those promises were fulfilled with the first coming of Christ. But it is none the less true that we still await their perfect fulfillment in His glorious return at the end of time.

Obviously, one cannot alter the text of the Bible. The point is that, with a version destined for liturgical use, there should be an overriding preoccupation to bring out explicitly the meaning of a text, while taking scriptural studies into account. Thus the formula 'the Jews,' in St. John, sometimes according to the context means 'the leaders of the Jews,' or 'the adversaries of Jesus,' terms which express better the thought of the evangelist and avoid appearing to arraign the Jewish people as such.

Jesus was born of the Jewish people as were His Apostoles and a large number of His first disciples. When He revealed Himself as the Messiah and Son of God . . . the bearer of the new Gospel message, He did so as the fulfillment and perfection of the earlier which he found himself in agreement.

Whenever He opposed it, it was always from within the Jewish people, just as did the prophets before Him.

The history of Judaism does not end with the destruction of Jerusalem, but continues to develop in a rich spiritual tradition.

According to New Testament teaching, the Jewish people play an essential role in the eschatological fulfillment of history.

Revelation. And, although His teaching had a profoundly new character, Christ, nevertheless, in many instances, took His stand on the teaching of the Old Testament. The New Testament is profoundly marked by its relation to the Old. As the Second Vatican Council declared: "God, the inspirer and author of the books of both Testaments, wisely arranged that the New Testament be hidden in the Old and the Old be made manifest in the New." . . . Jesus also used teaching methods similar to those employed by the rabbis of His time.

This history of Judaism did not end with the destruction of Jerusalem, but rather went on to develop a religious tradition. And, although we believe that the importance and meaning of that tradition were deeply affected by the coming of Christ, it is still nonetheless rich in religious values.

With the prophets and the Apostle Paul, "the Church awaits the day, known to God alone, on which all people will address the Lord in a single voice and 'serve Him with one accord' (Soph. 3:9)." (*Nostra Aetate*, 4)

The change in emphasis, although not in direction, from the first document is striking and obvious. But the very recasting illustrates our point that the Jewish-Christian encounter makes one evaluate very carefully one's Christological formulae and claims. Apparently, those who revised the Working Document felt that certain Christological formulae were too weak, ambiguous, or deficient in expressing orthodox belief in Christ. Further, in one place at least, the Commission linked a revision (cf. last paragraph cited) to the meaning of post-Jerusalem Judaism.

While neither the Working Document nor the Guidelines go so far as to admit Judaism's continuing validity, each asserts that the promises of God continue and that the Word of God is the source of Jewish vitality even today. One risks reading too much into the wording-changes between the two documents, but it cannot be denied that the former document was less qualified in certain statements: e.g., the former spoke of the Old Testament's "validity," the latter of "whatever in the Old Testament retains its perpetual value"; the second document dropped "rich" in describing the Jewish religious tradition after Jerusalem and omitted asserting "an essential role [for the Jews] in the eschatological fulfillment of history."

In the opening paragraph of the Guidelines, the authors felt that an expression of the traditional belief in Christ as fulfillment of the Old Testament prophecies was needed; nevertheless, the nature of this fulfillment is less than complete because perfect fulfillment comes only "at the end of time." The authors were chary about altering any translation of the Bible, even those destined for liturgical use. The Guidelines boldly assert that Jesus "revealed Himself as the Messiah and Son of God" —much stronger and more objective than claiming that Christ "presented Himself . . . as fulfilling the interior Revelation."

The Guidelines also emphasize, more than the Working Document, the points of divergence between Jesus and Judaism, although they admit the wide area of agreement. The text on Judaism's meaning after Christ in the Guidelines is a bit ambiguous, but its direction from that of the Working Document is clear—a more qualified affirming of Judaism's continuing religious validity. The Guidelines also shy away from affirming anything about an essential eschatological role for Israel; it reverts to a quotation from the Old Testament about the eschatological reunion.

Cautious the Guidelines are, but, nevertheless, a step beyond the conciliar documents.

2. Statements of Other Christian Churches, Groups, or Organizations

In 1947, the International Council of Christians and Jews sponsored the "Special Conference to Combat Anti-Semitism" at Seelisberg, Switzerland. According to *SIDIC*, a journal concerned with Jewish-Christian relations, "up to the time of Vatican Council II this [the "Ten Points of Seelisberg"] was the only international document to which Christians could refer to create a new climate."[46] As a background to official Protestant statements concerning the relation of Christians to Judaism, we quote from the Seelisberg document the sections appropriate to our subject:

1. Remember that One God speaks to us all through the Old and the New Testaments.

2. Remember that Jesus was born of a Jewish mother of the seed of David and the people of Israel, and that His everlasting love and forgiveness embrace His own people and the whole world.

3. Remember that the first disciples, the apostles and the first martyrs were Jews.

4. Remember that the fundamental commandment of Christianity, to love God and one's neighbour, proclaimed already in the Old Testament and confirmed by Jesus, is binding upon both Christians and Jews in all human relationships, without exception.

5. Avoid disparaging biblical or post-biblical Judaism with the object of extolling Christianity.[47]

These same themes appear in later Roman Catholic statements (cf. fn. 32 in this chapter) and occur in the following Protestant statements.

46. *SIDIC* 3 (1970):#2:3.
47. *Ibid.*, pp. 3-4.

a. *"Faith and Order Paper #50:*
   The Church and the Jewish People, 1967"[48]

In 1967, soon after the Roman Catholic Church promulgated its statement on the relation of the Church to the Jewish
people, the World Council of Churches issued a paper entitled
"The Church and the Jewish People." More extensive than the
Vatican II document, the WCC's statement sought to head off
any justification for antisemitic doctrine or action, while at the
same time reflecting on what theological significance the continued existence of Judaism might have for the Church. The sections which pertain to Christology are presented here:

[The text begins with historical considerations that the first
community of Christians were Jews, but after the break
with the synagogue, theological reflection on the Jews was
quite stylized:]

Christians generally thought about these questions in very
stereotyped ways: the Jews as the Israel of the Old Testament had formerly been God's elect people, but this election had been transferred to the Church after Christ; the
continuing existence of the Jews was primarily thought of
in terms of divine rejection and retribution, because they
were regarded as those who had killed Christ and whose
hearts were so hardened that they continued to reject him.

[Following the historical considerations are theological
considerations:]

We believe that in Jesus Christ God's revelation in the Old
Testament finds its fulfillment. Through him we see into
the very heart of God, in him we see what it really means
to say that God is the God of the Covenant and loves man
to the very end. As he became the man who was the perfect
instrument of God's purpose, he took upon himself the

48. Text from *Faith and Order Studies, 1964-1967* (Geneva: World Council of Churches, 1968), pp. 70-80.

vocation of his people. He, as its representative, fulfills Israel's task of obedience. In his resurrection it has become manifest that God's love is stronger than human sin. In him God has forgiven and wiped out sin and in him he created his true covenant-partner. . . . And together with Israel the Gentiles too were now called to the love and service of God. It cannot be otherwise; for if in Jesus Christ the fulness of time has really come, then the separation of Israel is abolished. This is what the Church is: Israel having come to recognize God in Christ, together with the Gentiles who are engrafted into Israel, so that now Jew and Gentile become one in Christ. It is only in this way that the Church is the continuation of the Israel of the Old Testament, God's chosen people, called upon to testify to his mighty acts for men, and to be his fellow-workers in this world. Christ himself is the ground and substance of this continuity. This is underlined by the preservation of the Old Testament in the Church as an integral part of her worship and tradition. . . . We are convinced that the Jewish people still have a significance of their own for the Church. It is not merely that by God's grace they have preserved in their faith truths and insights into his revelation which we have tended to forget . . . it seems to us that by their very existence in spite of all attempts to destroy them, they make it manifest that God has not abandoned them. In this way they are a living and visible sign of God's faithfulness to men, an indication that he also upholds those who do not find it possible to recognize him in his Son. While we see their continuing existence as pointing to God's love and mercy, we explicitly reject any thought of considering their sufferings during the ages as proof of any special guilt.

It is true that we believe that Jesus Christ is the truth and the way for every man, and that for everyone faith in him is salvation. But we also know that it is only by grace that we have come to accept him and that even in our acceptance we are still in many ways disobedient. We have therefore no reason to pride ourselves over against others. For Christians as well as Jews can live only by the forgiveness of sin, and by God's mercy. . . . So long as the Jews do not worship with the Church the one God and Father of Jesus Christ, they are to us a perpetual reminder that God's purpose and promise are not yet realized in their fulness, and that we have still much to hope for the world, looking for the time when the Kingdom of God will become plainly and gloriously manifest.

[The statement goes on to describe the abiding disagreement which the authors have concerning the theological identity of Israel; in brief, the positions are:]

Some are convinced that . . . to speak of the continued election of the Jewish people alongside the Church is inadmissible. It is the Church alone, they say, that is, theologically speaking, the continuation of Israel as the people of God, to which now all nations belong. Elections and vocation are solely in Christ, and are to be grasped in faith. To speak otherwise is to deny that the one people of God, the Church, is the body of Christ which cannot be broken . . . the Christian hope for the Jews is the same as it is for all men: That they may come to the knowledge of the truth, Jesus Christ our Lord.

Others [assert] . . . that they [the Jewish people] actually are still Israel, i.e., that they still are God's elect people. These would stress that after Christ the one people of God is broken asunder, one part being the Church which accepts Christ, the other part Israel outside the Church, which rejects him, but which even in this rejection remains in a special sense beloved by God. . . . Further they see this continuing election in the fact that God has linked the final hope of the world to the salvation of the Jews, in the day when he will heal the broken body of his one people, Israel and the Church.

The conversation among us has only just begun and we realize that in this question the entire self-understanding of the Church is at stake.

[Closely allied with these Christological considerations are differences in ecclesiologies:]

If the main emphasis is put on the concept of the Church as the body of Christ, the Jewish people are seen as being outside. . . . Those who hold this view would generally want to stress that besides service to the Jews it is also legitimate and even necessary to witness in a more explicit way as well, be it through individuals or special societies or churches.

If, on the other hand, the Church is primarily seen as the people of God, it is possible to regard the Church and the Jewish people together as forming the one people of God. . . . Those who follow this line of thinking would say that the Church should consider her attitude towards the Jews theologically and in principle as being different from the attitude she has to all other men who do not believe in Christ. It should be thought of more in terms of ecumenical engagement in order to heal the breach than of missionary witness in which she hopes for conversion.[49]

The candor with which the issues and disagreements are described is quite remarkable. Where the Roman Church strove for unanimity, the Protestant, Anglican, and Orthodox Churches represented in the WCC achieved breadth and completeness. All the major issues which challenge the Jewish-Christian encounter (except the state of Israel), especially those which force Christian reassessment of doctrinal belief and formulation, are given equal and positive hearing. The statement links together very closely the Christological and ecclesiological issues. Although preliminary resolution on some points was achieved, a sharp disagreement was articulated on the contem-

49. *Ibid.*, pp. 70-76. Quoted by permission.

porary theological identity and validity of Judaism and the appropriate ecclesiological model for Christians in the Jewish-Christian dialogue. The statement reads more as an agenda for further discussion than as a position paper of current self-understanding.

b. *"The Church and the Jewish People"*[50]

The following text from the Lutheran World Federation represents a document at least five years in the making. Within the document itself, a shift of emphasis occurs—from an articulation of, and insistence upon, the absolute fulfillment of Jesus and the necessity of mission to the Jews, to a self-critical acknowledgement of some harsh differences between Judaism and Christianity. Also, classic Lutheran themes—salvation through grace and gospel/law dichotomy—inform this self-scrutiny vis-à-vis the Jewish people. Again, pertinent sections are quoted here, noting the different years of composition:

[1964] Thus the Church testifies that, by the fulfillment of the promises in Jesus the Messiah and by his acceptance by but a part of the Jews, a division has arisen which has placed the 'old' Israel outside the 'new.' This division will be healed when 'all Israel' (Rom. 11:26) recognizes Jesus of Nazareth as its Messiah. . . .

The witness to the Jewish people is inherent in the content of the gospel, and in the commission received from Christ, the head of the Church. The mission will most effectively reflect the glory of Christ in his gospel when it is pursued in the normal activity of the Christian congregation, which reflects itself in the Christian witness of the individual members.

50. Prepared in 1964 and 1969 by various committees on the Church and the Jews, at the request of the Lutheran World Federation. Text from *Speaking of God Today: Jews and Lutherans in Dialogue*, pp. 166-173, edited by Paul Opsahl and Marc Tanenbaum (Philadelphia: Fortress Press, 1974).

[1969] As Lutherans we believe, on the basis of Paul's witness, that it is God's action in Christ which justifies the sinner. Thus we cannot speak about the law and about righteousness as though it were obedience which lays the foundation for relationship to God. . . . Our understanding can be traced to Luther and his reception through Augustine of certain Pauline motifs. It is possible, however, that our whole outlook has been shaped and our relationship to the Jewish people has been vitiated by a strongly negative understanding of the Law and its function.

The faith and the universal proclamation that God became man, that God was in Christ reconciling the world unto himself, that Jesus of Nazareth was the Son of God, is an offense to human wisdom and particularly to the religious view of God's glory. It is as if God had of necessity to meet rejection and to suffer the consequences of his love in order to bring life and salvation to mankind. . . . Because Jesus took upon himself his cross and became obedient unto death, God raised him from the dead. His death and resurrection constitute a special Christian hope for the whole world. This implies the crucial paradox that for the Christian faith there is a divine future for mankind since Jesus the Nazarene was rejected. . . . Mystery and paradox—the point where human logic leads no further—stand at the center of all Christian thought. That is the case with Christology, but it is equally true of eschatology, and it applies to ecclesiology as well. . . . It is our conviction that the central position of the cross and resurrection of Jesus has fundamental consequences for the understanding of the Church. This was perceived and expressed in a unique way by Luther. He did not accept identification of the elect people of God with a specific ecclesiological tradition. . . .

We assert our Christian responsibility for their right to exist as Jews. Jews, on their side, insist that there can be mutual respect and dialogue only if the 'legitimacy' of Judaism is recognized by Christians. . . . What does it mean for us to acknowledge its 'legitimacy'? . . . Does affirmation of the survival or acknowledgment of the legitimacy of Judaism cancel the responsibility of the Christian to bear witness to the Jew at the right time and in the proper way?

We as Lutherans affirm our solidarity with the Jewish people. This solidarity is legitimized in God's election and calling into being in Abraham's seed a people of promise. . . . The Lutheran Churches, therefore, may not so appropriate the term 'people of God' and 'Israel' to the Church in such a way as to deny that they applied in the first instance to the Jewish people. They may not assert that continuity of the church with the covenant people of Abraham in such a way as to question the fact that present-day Judaism has its own continuity with the Old Testament Israel. . . .

Whenever we Christians, therefore, speak about 'rejection' and 'faith,' 'disobedience' and 'obedience,' in such a way that 'rejection' and 'disobedience' are made to be attributes of Jews while 'faith' and 'obedience' are made to be attributes of Christians, we are not only guilty of the most despicable spiritual pride, but we foster a pernicious slander, denying the very ground of our own existence: grace, forgiveness, and justification.

In understanding ourselves as people of the new covenant which God has made in Jesus the Christ, we Christians see the Jewish people as a reminder of our origin, as a partner in dialogue to understand our common history, and as a living admonition that we too are a pilgrim people, a people en-route toward a goal that can only be grasped in hope.

This message shows forth a time when God's purpose with his covenant in Abraham and with his covenant in Jesus the Christ will be fulfilled. Then God overcomes all blindness, faithlessness, and disobedience and will be all in all.[51]

The earlier part of the document affirms the universal claim on all persons to believe in Christ, with the consequent obligation of the Church to preach Christ to all nations: Christ is the fulfillment of the promises, thus the Messiah. An interesting development in this particular document is the inclusion of the Christian profession of belief in the resurrection of Christ with the characteristically Lutheran emphases on grace, paradox, and the cross. Further, the Christology affirmed allows the Jewish people "theological room" to hold onto their election and cautions the Lutheran Church from using typically supersessionist phrases like "new people of God" and "new Israel." The last section assumes that Lutheran Christology provides for a non-exclusivist position vis-à-vis the Jews; what binds Christians and Jews together are not only the positive common possessions—their common history, their solidarity in God's election and a continuity of the Church with the covenant people of Abraham—but also their mutual sinfulness. The document seems, in the last paragraph, to employ some kind of "double-covenant" theory.[52]

c. *"A Statement on Interreligious Dialogue: Jews and Christians, 1972"*[53]

The product of the Executive Committee of the United Methodist Church's General Commission on Ecumenical Affairs, the "Statement on Interreligious Dialogue: Jews and Christians" is a first attempt by Methodists to enter the Jewish-Christian dialogue. Striving primarily for mutual understanding

51. *Ibid.*, pp. 166-167, 169-173. Quoted by permission.
52. In 1971, the Lutheran Council in the United States prepared "Some Observations and Guidelines for Conversations between Lutherans and Jews" as a practical follow-up to the statement just examined. For the text, see *Speaking of God Today*, pp. 163-165, edited by Paul Opsahl.
53. Adopted by the General Conference of the United Methodist Church, Atlanta, Georgia, April 1972.

which will hopefully result from the ensuing conversation, the document speaks little of Christ:

> The United Methodist Church understands itself to be part of the People of God and specifically a part of the whole Christian Church, the Body of Christ. It also gives thanks for its roots in historic Judaism. . . . The heritage and hopes of an Israel in the context of which Jesus labored have continued to live in the Jewish faith and people. . . . Moreover, to be faithful to Jesus the Jew, the contemporary relationship of United Methodist Christians and those who worship as Jews should not be neglected.
>
> The relationship between the covenant of God with Israel and the covenant made in Jesus Christ and the understandings by Jew and Christian of each of these covenants merits exploration anew.
>
> Our intent includes commitment to their [Jews'] intrinsic worth and import for society. It includes as well the Christian hope that the 'oneness given in Jesus Christ' may become an example of hope for the oneness of humanity.[54]

In contrast to the Faith and Order consideration of conflicting ecclesiologies, one might infer from the Methodist statement that the Body of Christ is the Christians' part of the larger People of God. Secondly, there is foundation for, though hardly definition of, a two-covenant theory—one with Israel and one made in Jesus Christ. Emphasis on the Jewishness of Jesus is also evident.

In the light of these preliminary directions, the Methodist statement provides the groundwork for a faith in Christ which does not, at the same time, negate the worth of contemporary Jewish religious experience.

54. *Ibid.*

d. *"The American Lutheran Church
and the Jewish Community, 1974"*[55]

In response to a 1972 request for a statement of the American Lutheran Church on its relation to Jews, a number of Lutheran theologians prepared a statement which was made public at the 1974 convention of the American Lutheran Church. Understanding the relation of the Lutherans to Jews to be one "of solidarity, of confrontation and of respect and cooperation," the document made the following Christological assertions:

It is important to note that the ministry of Jesus and the life of the early Christian community were thoroughly rooted in the Judaism of their day. To emphasize the Jewishness of Jesus and his disciples, and to stress all that binds Jews and Christians together in their mutual history is also to attack one of the sources of anti-Jewish prejudice.

Judaism, while it does indeed have teachings, differs markedly from Christian denominations in that its essence is best summed up not in a set of beliefs or creeds, but in a way of life.

For Lutherans as well, the Hebrew Scriptures do not have independent authority. They gain their significance from their role as *Old* Testament and are subordinated to the New Testament Christ, in whom they find a complex fulfillment, involving cancellation as well as acceptance, and reinterpretation as well as reaffirmation. . . . The consequence of this is that Lutherans must view Judaism as a religion with which we in part agree wholeheartedly and yet in part disagree emphatically. Judaism worships the same God as we do (the God of Abraham is our God), yet it disavows the Christ in whom, according to Christian faith, all God's promises have their fulfillment and through whom God has revealed the fullness of his grace.

55. Text from the *1974 Reports and Actions, Part 2*, of the *Seventh General Convention of the American Lutheran Church*, pp. 752-757.

Many Lutherans wish to engage in a mutual sharing of convictions, not only for the sake of greater maturity, but also because Christian faith is marked by the impulse to bear witness through word and deed to the grace of God in Jesus Christ.

[Admitting the disagreement among Lutherans:] Some Lutherans find in Scripture clear directives to bear missionary witness in which conversion is hoped for. Others hold that when Scripture speaks about the relation between Jews and Christians its central theme is that God's promises to Israel have not been abrogated. The one approach desires to bring Jews into the body of Christ, while the other tends to see the church and the Jewish people as together forming the one people of God, separated from one another for the time being, yet with the promise that they will ultimately become one.

It would be too simple to apply the labels 'mission' and 'dialogue' to these points of view, although in practice some will want to bear explicit witness. . . . Witness, whether it be called 'mission' or 'dialogue,' includes a desire both to know and to be known more fully.[56]

This statement speaks at length to the Lutheran community about the nature of the Jewish religion and its difference from the Christian understanding of "denomination" or "faith community." Furthermore, the statement goes farther than others we have examined in describing the place of the Scriptures in the Jewish tradition as analogous to the subordinate position which the Old Testament has with reference to the New Testament in the Christian tradition. Also this statement, in contrast to the former Lutheran statement, further distinguishes mission from polemics and conversions. Like the Faith and Order document, the American Lutheran Church points out two

56. *Ibid.*, pp. 753-756; commenting on the document referred to in fn. 52 above, "Some Observations," this document from the American Lutheran Church states that the former's "comment that 'neither polemics nor conversions are the aim of such conversations' does not rule out mission" (p. 756).

divergent ecclesiological positions affecting Jewish-Christian dialogue rather than settling for either.

C.
SUMMARY

The following Christological drifts may be noted in the major statements by the Christian Church on the nature of the relationship between Church and the Jewish people.

Every statement underscored the fact that Jesus was Jewish, that he could only be understood as standing in a religiously Jewish milieu.[57] Although many mentioned that Jesus was the fulfillment of the Old Testament prophecies and of Israel's hopes for a Messiah, the later documents tended to speak of partial fulfillment in Jesus and complete fulfillment only in the end times—which fulfillment is the object of both Christian and Jewish messianic hopes. None of the statements claimed a complete break from the Jewish religion, but saw rather in Jesus a new beginning or a new covenant; if this beginning did not abrogate the former covenant, much less did it mean that God had withdrawn his special love for the Jewish people. A few statements candidly linked Christologies which emphasize faith in Jesus as the absolute past fulfillment of messianic prophecies and salvation only through explicit faith in him (sometimes referred to as "exclusivist" or "absolutist" Christologies) with certain ecclesiologies, e.g., the Church as the Body of Christ. Some seemed to acknowledge Jesus as the sole mediator of salvation, yet tried to leave theological room for the abiding validity of Judaism, while at the same time refrained from delineating how these beliefs might co-exist. Allied with these considerations was the effort on the part of many documents to recognize the validity of the Hebrew Scriptures in themselves and not only as related to, interpreted by, or preparatory to full revelation in Jesus.

---

57. "For centuries, neither Christianity nor Judaism had come to terms with the fact that Jesus was a Jew. Christians failed to understand why he should have come out of Judaism, while Jews tended to ignore Jesus, and his significance for world history": Eva Fleischner, *Judaism*, p. 126, quoted by permission.

Noteworthy omissions (for the most part) were references to the resurrection (a central focus of contemporary Christology) and the divinity of Christ; there were relatively few references to Christ as Messiah. In the later documents, there also seemed to be a conscious effort to avoid supersessionist-tending language.

These minimal positive Christological claims by Christians in the Jewish-Christian encounter stand starkly against the more absolutist claims of Church documents not concerned with the Jewish question. For example, one need read only a few paragraphs of the Second Vatican Council's decree on ecumenism or on missionary activity to see the difference in Christological claims.

It is now time to focus on what Christian theologians involved in, and concerned with, Jewish-Christian relations are saying about their Christological understanding in their encounter with Judaism.

III
A Survey of
Scholarly Theological Opinion

One finds the root model for dialogue in the face-to-face conversation of two people. Ideally, of course, this sort of dialogue is what the Jewish-Christian dialogue aims for—the conversation of committed Christians and Jews in their mutual search for deeper self-understanding, and appreciation and understanding of the other. Nonetheless, a large part of the record of the Jewish-Christian dialogue is to be found in a more formal forum than the over-the-table discussions and in less official statements than Church documents. Therefore in the first part of this chapter, we will be dealing with official dialogues, which dialogues, however, do not result in Church statements. In the second part of this chapter, we will look at another primary source for the progress and content of the Jewish-Christian dialogue: the public forum of theological writings. In both parts, we will note the drifts and threads of Christologies which, explicitly or implicitly, are operative.

A.
FORMAL DIALOGUES

Formal dialogues between Jews and Christians are only in their infancy stages of development. The urgency for such formal dialogues is lukewarm at best—for many reasons. On the Jewish side, the assessment of the need for such conversation is mixed; indeed, many conservative and almost all orthodox Jews refrain from such dialogues. All too suspicious of the Christian penchant for proselytizing, some Jews question the motive of

Christians who initiate such dialogue. On the Christian side, it is only within the last few years that churches have begun to rethink systematically Judaism as a valid religious expression today and only recently have the churches assumed a posture of dialogue vis-à-vis Judaism. It is not surprising, then, that the churches' initial efforts have been to issue statements about Christianity's relation to Judaism to their own constituents. It is equally not surprising that dialogue itself, in a formal setting, is only in its infancy stage. Nevertheless, there have been some advances made and these will be the focus of this section of our study—formal dialogues and the Christologies at work in them.[1]

1. *"Israel: Land, People, State"*[2]

Drawn up by a group of eighteen Catholic, Protestant, and Orthodox theologians, "Israel: Land, People, State" proposes to be a "theological statement," with concrete ramifications, of Jewish-Christian relations. Those parts which pertain to Christology are presented here:

> The Church of Christ is rooted in the life of the People of Israel. We Christians look upon Abraham as our spiritual ancestor and father of our faith. . . . The ministry of Jesus

1. Admittedly, choosing which statements belong to this category is somewhat arbitrary; we exclude those books which are made up of essays by noted theologians on Jewish-Christian relations (e.g., Philip Scharper's *Torah and Gospel*, John Oesterreicher's *Brothers in Hope*, etc.)—the articles contained in those collections will be considered in the following section, "Informal Dialogues." Here we will examine the record of those dialogues drawn up by officially designated Christian bodies, which have been issued and written by theologians, not as a statement of policy or position (in contrast to Chapter II), but as contributions to the ongoing dialogue. After careful and extensive bibliographical research, we have come up with only two such contributions— "Israel: People, Land, State" (1973) issued by the National Catholic-Protestant Theological Dialogue, and the records of the Lutheran-Jewish Dialogue.

2. Written by the National Catholic-Protestant Theological Dialogue, sponsored by the Commission on Faith and Order of the National Council of Churches and the Secretariat for Catholic-Jewish Relations of the National Conference for Catholic Bishops, issued June 19, 1973.

and the life of the early Christian community were thoroughly rooted in the Judaism of their day, particularly in the teachings of the Pharisees. The Christian Church is still sustained by the living faith of the patriarchs and prophets, kings and priests, scribes and rabbis, and the people whom God chose for his own. Christ is the link . . . enabling the Gentiles to be numbered among Abraham's 'offspring' and therefore fellow-heirs with the Jews according to God's promise. It is a tragedy of history that Jesus, our bond of unity with the Jews, has all too often become a symbol and source of division and bitterness because of human weakness and pride.

The singular grace of Jesus Christ does not abrogate the covenantal relationship of God with Israel. . . . In Christ the Church shares in Israel's election without superseding it. . . . The survival of the Jewish people . . . is a sign of God's continuing fidelity to the people dear to him. For our spiritual legacy and for all that the Jews have done for the whole human race we Christians are grateful to God and to the people whom God has chosen as a special instrument of his kindness.

We Christians have readily acknowledged that God made a covenant with the Jews in the past, promising his paternal care for his chosen people in return for their fidelity. Unfortunately many Christians have assumed that the validity of Judaism ended with the beginning of Christianity, the rejection of Jesus as Messiah marking the dissolution of the covenant. This assumption conflicts sharply with St. Paul's declaration that God did not annul his promise to the chosen people since God never takes back his gifts or revokes his call. . . . The Apostle dismissed as altogether untenable the notion that God has rejected his people. There is thus strong Scriptural support for the position that God's covenant love for the Jewish people remains firm. The continuity of contemporary Judaism with ancient

Israel demonstrates the abiding validity of Jewish worship
and life as authentic forms of service to the true God.[3]

Like some of the official statements before it, "Israel: People, Land, State" begins by rooting the Christian faith in the
religion of Israel. Unlike the former statements, however, this
statement denies a single Judaeo-Christian tradition; rather it
offers "the recognition that two religious traditions . . . have
shaped our culture." Like some of the official statements, this
statement underscores the Jewishness of Jesus. James Will,
commenting on this aspect of the statement, feels that the truth
of this emphasis is not the whole picture, for Jesus also tran-
scended history: "Thus he was surely Jewish man, but Jewish
man pointing the way toward community with all men, and thus
he was in some sense the Son of Man or simply Man as such."[4]

Further, the present statement explicitly repudiates any supersessionist doctrine while trying to maintain the uniqueness of
the "singular grace of Jesus Christ." At the same time the statement explicitly repudiates any Christology which would understand that the Jewish covenant has been invalidated since
Christ's coming. In this sense the Christology operative here
seems to be a negative one; that is, whatever Christians believe
about Christ cannot mean that the Jews have been abandoned
by God, nor has God ceased to bless Jewish worship as an abiding expression and place of his blessing.[5]

3. *Ibid.*

4. James Will, "A Response to 'A Statement to Our Fellow Christians' "
[mimeograph], 1973.

5. Greek Orthodox Robert C. Stephanopoulos, "Observations on 'A
Statement to Our Fellow Christians,' " thought that the assertion of the continuing validity of Jewish worship "can only be understood in terms of the
fullness of God's revelation in Jesus Christ, as a form of temporal or existential
preparation for the new (read 'transforming') covenant in Christ. Therefore,
contemporary Judaism is *essentially* no different than other living religions in
relation to Christianity" [mimeograph], 1973. It is interesting to note that the
two criticisms we have cited find fault with the statement only with regard to the
inadequacy of the Christology contained therein.

2. *The Lutheran-Jewish Dialogue*

For many years, the Lutheran Church in the United States has sought mutual understanding with the Jewish people through dialogues and reports. As far back as 1954, the Lutherans have addressed themselves to the question of the Church's relationship to the Jews; the results of these initial probings were the Evanston Report (1954), which began with the assertion: "Jesus Christ is the Savior of all mankind." The Report went on to note the Hebrew patrimony of the Christian Church. The core of that document claims a requirement that eventually all Jews must become Christian:

The New Testament, however, speaks also of the 'fullness' of Israel, when God will manifest his glory by bringing back his 'eldest son' into the one fold of his grace (Romans 11:12-36; Matthew 23:29). This belief is an indispensable element of our one united hope for Jew and Gentile in Jesus Christ. Our hope in Christ's coming victory includes our hope for Israel in Christ, in his victory over the blindness of his own people. To expect Jesus Christ means to hope for the conversion of the Jewish people, and to love the people of God's promise.[6]

Not until the Lutheran World Federation's Department of World Mission met at Løgumkloster, Denmark, in 1964, did further development occur on a corporate level (see appropriate sections quoted in the previous chapter). The focus of some subsequent meetings has been to expunge from Lutheran teaching materials all antisemitic references. Many local efforts at dialogue and mutual understanding took place, but Lutherans on the national level were seeking a forum for conversations that were basically *theological* in character. In cooperation with the Anti-Defamation League and the American Jewish Committee, the Division of Theological Studies of the Lutheran World Federation has sponsored four colloquia on the following topics:

6. "The Evanston Report (1954)," text from the *Lutheran World* 11 (1964):358. Quoted by permission.

"Law and Grace" and "Election and the People of God" (New York City, 1969); "Promise, Land, Peoplehood (St. Louis, 1971; "The State and Religious Community" (Brandeis University, 1971); "How We Speak of God Today—in an Age of Pluralism, in an Age of Technology, after Auschwitz" (Columbus, Ohio, 1973).

The contents of these conversations have recently been published in one volume.[7] However because this volume is a collection of essays expressing the opinions of individual theologians, the essays would be more fruitfully treated in the following section designated "Informal Dialogues." Nevertheless, the uniqueness of the Lutheran effort should not be underestimated. While other Christian bodies have issued statements and while other independent groups have arranged theological colloquia, only the Lutherans, as a group, have sponsored ongoing theological conversations with Jews.

B.
"INFORMAL DIALOGUES":
THE THEOLOGIANS—AN ANALYTICAL BREAKDOWN

Up to now we have concentrated on the Christological assertions of Christian bodies in the Jewish-Christian encounter. For the most part these assertions have been the result of consensus, or they have been honest descriptions of positions which fall short of consensus. On the vanguard of religious thinking, however, are the Christian theologians concerned with Jewish-Christian relations.

Some theologians, persuaded of the radical difference between the Jewish and Christian traditions, claim that there is no possibility for a "bridge theology," while at the same time they deplore antisemitism and call for a Christian appreciation of the

7. *Speaking of God Today: Jews and Lutherans in Conversation*, edited by Paul D. Opsahl and Marc H. Tanenbaum (Philadelphia: Fortress Press, 1974); for the records of previous Lutheran reflections on the relation of Christianity to Judaism, see *Lutheran World* 10 (1963):345-408; 11 (1964):261-358. For reports on the above-mentioned colloquia, see *Lutheran Quarterly* 21 (1969):401-459, 501; *JES* 8 (1971):497-499, 9 (1972):448-450.

Jewish heritage. Others articulate a "bridge theology" which maintains the theological integrity and validity of both religious traditions. Many locate the foundation for their bridge theology on a proper understanding of Jesus Christ, although some see other issues to be the lynchpin for understanding the Jewish-Christian relationship. Variously stated, the claim is made that the cornerstone of Jewish-Christian relations involves a proper understanding of revelation, covenant, election, Trinity, Messiahship, or the nature of religious language.[8]

While it would be profitable to follow out each of these suggestions, our concern is with how the theologians interested in the Jewish-Christian encounter have expressed their understanding of Christ. As an analytic tool in our investigation, we will adapt the schema which A. Roy Eckardt, in his *Elder Brother, Younger Brother,*[9] used to describe theologies that account for the relationship between Judaism and Christianity— theologies of discontinuity and continuity.

The theology of discontinuity, applied to Christology, stresses the uniqueness and finality of Christ; the universality of Christ as the sole mediator of salvation; Christ as the fulfillment of Jewish hopes and prophecies; Christ as the leader and embodiment of the New Israel, successor to Judaism; Christ as Messiah; and the necessity of preaching Christ to the Jewish people. The theology of continuity, applied to Christology, stresses Christianity as the continuation of Israel's covenant

---

8. Locating the issue in the notion of revelation, see Peter Chirico, "Christian and Jew Today from a Theological Perspective, *JES* 7 (1970):37-51 and J. Coert Rylaarsdsdam, "Jewish-Christian Relationship: The Two Covenants and the Dilemmas of Christology," *JES* 9 (1972):249-270; in election, Frank M. Cross, Jr., "A Christian Understanding of the Election of Israel," in *The Death of Dialogue and Beyond*, pp. 72-85, edited by Sanford Seltzer and Max L. Stackhouse (New York: Friendship Press, 1969) and Alan T. Davies, "The Jews in an Ecumenical Context," *JES* 5 (1968):496; in the Trinity, James Parkes, *Prelude to Dialogue*, p. 200; in the notion of Messiahship, Rosemary Radford Ruether, "An Invitation to Jewish-Christian Dialogue: In What Sense Can We Say That Jesus was 'The Christ'?" *The Ecumenist* 10 (1972):17-24 and Frederick C. Grant, *Ancient Judaism and the New Testament*, p. 22; in the nature of religious language, Gregory Baum, "The Jews, Faith and Ideology," *The Ecumenist* 10 (1971-1972):71-76, esp. pp. 75ff, and Monika Hellwig, "Christian Theology," pp. 50f.

9. pp. 50f.

which Christ does not abrogate, but which he opens up to the Gentile world. This Christology speaks of the abiding validity of the covenant with Israel; the positive witness of the Jewish "no" to Jesus; the positive Jewish witness to the unredeemed character of the world; Christ as *partial* fulfillment of Jewish messianic prophecies; and the eschatological unification of all God's peoples.

Obviously, this breakdown is inadequate to account strictly for all positions espoused by Christians in the Jewish-Christian encounter.[10] Many will be the points of overlap, but in the main there is a certain validity to this breakdown which we hope to illustrate below.

Necessarily the second category (Christologies of continuity) will be more variegated and nuanced. This is so, not only because the subject matter demands it, but simply because there are more positions to be considered there. It should be noted, too, that the number of theologians cited under the first category is appreciably fewer than those in the second. The reason for this is that Christian thinkers tending to hold the first position have less reason to write about the Jewish-Christian encounter. For them, the Jews are not a special case of non-Christians in the universal mission of the Church; nor does the fact of continued Jewish existence pose any question about their own theological positions or presuppositions. The call of Christ is universal, and therefore applies without discrimination to all peoples, including the Jews. Antisemitism is only one expression of sinful man's failing to love his neighbor—for them, the roots of antisemitism have as little foundation in Christian theology as any other racism. Nevertheless, there are some Christian thinkers, moved by contrition at Christian antisemitism, who have investigated the Jewish-Christian question and have arrived at a Christology of discontinuity. These thinkers are our first focus among the theologians in the "informal dialogues."

10. Eckardt's position itself is in his 1967 book one of a tension between continuity and discontinuity, stressing the former. See *ibid.*, p. 160.

1. *Christologies of Discontinuity*[11]

Long-standing writer and authority on Jewish-Christian relationships, *Jakob Jocz* delivered a series of lectures in 1965 at
Princeton University where he noted with appreciation the debt
which Christianity owes to the Jewish people. But in those lectures he warned that the encounter with modern-day Judaism
must not tempt Christians to accommodate the Synagogue in
their Christology.[12] Noting the tendency of modern Christian
theologians to speak of Messianic claims only in terms of eschatological fulfillment, Jocz scores such adjustment as compromise. Rather:

> [Christ is] the kind of Messiah who directly contradicts
> Jewish messianic hopes. . . . Whenever the Church offers
> a more 'Jewish' answer [to the question 'Who is Christ?'],
> the Lordship of Jesus Christ becomes a special issue. The
> moment we profess Jesus Christ as Lord a missionary situ-
> ation is created.[13]

This position is the Christological conclusion of Jocz' previous books published in the late 1940's.[14] In these works, he
has given an extended history of the controversy between Judaism and Christianity. Jocz claimed that the chasm between
Judaism and Christianity was located precisely in Christology.

11. Among the theologians of discontinuity, Eckardt numbers (with quali-
fications) Karl Barth and Rudolf Bultmann (*ibid.*, pp. 52f, 58f). Since these
theologians wrote long before Vatican II, they are not our concern here, but
their mention is important because their thought has greatly influenced succeed-
ing Christian thinkers.

12. For a less harsh expression of the same position, see Joseph Estes,
"Jewish-Christian Dialogue as Mission," but interestingly, Estes grants that an
important principle of dialogue is to acknowledge Judaism as "a viable religious
reality which continues to be a valid expression of the covenant of God with
Israel of old . . . [which has a] continuing vocation . . . in the economy of
God" (p. 9).

13. "Jakob Jocz, *Christians and Jews: Encounter and Mission* (Naperville,
IL: Alec R. Allenson, Inc. Distributors: published by SPCK), pp. 40, 47. Quoted
by Permission."

14. *Idem, The Jewish People and Jesus Christ; A Theology of Election:
Israel and the Church* (London: SPCK, 1958).

For Christians to refrain from preaching Christ to the Jews is an act of unfaithfulness to the Christian message: "Between the Church and the Synagogue stands the Crucified. Church and Synagogue derive their existence from their attitude toward him."[15] While it is untrue to say that the Synagogue "derives" its existence from Christ, nevertheless Jocz expresses very clearly a theology of discontinuity with Judaism—so strongly expressed that he even admits that Jesus transforms, rather than fulfills, the Jewish concept of Messiah. Jocz' stance is professedly conversionist, and he would be hard pressed to offer any theological reason why Judaism has a right to exist other than as a preparation for Christianity.

In some ways, Jocz follows out to its logical conclusion some of the positions of those who stress discontinuity. For instance, in an essay aptly titled "Beyond Dialogue," *George A. F. Knight* concludes a rather sympathetic essay on the Jews with the injunction, "There is one thing, and only one thing, that we must communicate to Jews as to all men, and that is Christ. . . . [To do otherwise] is a form of religious anti-Semitism."[16] Knight, in previous essays in the same volume, stresses the absolute fulfillment of Old Testament prophecies about the Messiah in Jesus, so much so that Jesus himself is the new Israel: "Israel, as the elect people of God from of old, now finds her meaning and the 'end' of her own election in him,"[17] Admitting no other but a Christological understanding of the Old Testament, he defines the Jews as those people who do not *yet* believe in Jesus Christ. Knight can find no positive significance in the ᵗontinued existence of the Jews.

Other aspects of belief about Jesus which Knight emphasizes are Jesus' sinlessness, his fulfillment of Old Testament

15. *Idem, The Jewish People*, p. 264; see also pp. 320-322.
16. George A. F. Knight, "Beyond Dialogue," p. 175, in *Jews and Christians: Preparation for Dialogue*, edited by *idem* (Philadelphia: The Westminster Press, 1965).
17. *Idem*, "The 'Mystery' of Israel," p. 48, in *Jews and Christians*, edited by George A. F. Knight.

prophecies, the new covenant made in Him, and Christ as the "fullness of Israel's unbelief."[18]

Echoing this emphasis on the fulfillment of the Old Testament messianic prophecies in Jesus of Nazareth is the great French Catholic theologian *Jean Daniélou*. One of his lifelong projects was investigating, primarily from an historical viewpoint, the relationship of early Judaism to Christianity.[19] Subsequent writings have addressed more directly the contemporary Jewish-Christian relationship, including a very lively dialogue with the French Jewish scholar Andre Chouraqui.[20]

Jean Daniélou certainly does not tread lightly when he describes the relation between Judaism and Christianity:

> The offense [*peche*] of Israel is not that they crucified Jesus; it is that they did not believe in the risen Christ ... The true Israel continued in a small group of Jews who believed in the Christ.[21]

That God became man should be less a problem for the Jews than it is, according to Daniélou. Such a doctrine, he writes, is unthinkable for the Greeks, but not for the Jewish people—the history of the Jewish people is a history of a personal God in-

---

18. *Idem*, "Building Theological Bridges: I. The Incarnation," p. 123, in *Jews and Christians*; "The 'Mystery,' " pp. 48-53. By concentrating on Jesus' sinlessness, Knight intends to include the Jews with all others in the common denomination of sinfulness, and it is this characteristic which marks the Jewish people's need for Jesus. This racial and religious leveling is present in other evangelical writers. See, for example, Jacob Gartenhaus, "How To Approach the Jew with the Gospel," *Christianity Today* 11 (1966):253-255 (p. 255): "Christianity does not require the Jew to give up his Jewish heritage; it requires him only to give up his sins. All he has to do is to believe in the Jewish Messiah, as he is depicted in the Jewish Bible and revealed in the New Testament." One might speculate that the little regard for structure, for belonging to "the Church" among certain evangelicals would make them have less appreciation for the ethnically or nationally constituted self-consciousness of Judaism. Quoted by permission.

19. See Jean Daniélou, *The Theology of Jewish Christianity* (Chicago: Henry Regnery Co., 1964) and his *The Dead Sea Scrolls and Primitive Christianity* (Baltimore: Helicon Press, 1958).

20. Jean Daniélou and Andre Chouraqui, *The Jews: Views and Counterviews—A Dialogue* (New York: Newman Press, 1967).

21. Jean Daniélou, *Dialogue with Israel* (Baltimore: Helicon Press, 1966), p. 99, quoted by permission.

vesting himself in their history. Daniélou speaks not of two covenants but of the one covenant that has been enlarged to include all the nations in Christ. According to Daniélou, "it is certain . . . [that Christ] placed himself absolutely in a continuous line with the prophets of the Old Testament," and was the one foretold by Israel's prophets. It is for this reason, then, that it is difficult for the Christian to place the present-day Jewish people in his vision, for Christ is the one who "fully realized in himself all the messianic hopes." Since this is so, neither is the Jewish religion on an equal level with Christianity, nor can "we [Christians] . . . give up trying to convert you [Jews]."[22]

Daniélou certainly does not mince words in speaking with his Jewish dialogue partner, and, for that reason, Chouraqui is just as candid in denying that Jesus was the Messiah and that he was God. While Daniélou is unyielding in his absolute Christological claims, he does not refrain from dialogue—in fact, he seeks it out and, more interestingly, he does not try to "convert" Chouraqui in the discussion. Rather he talks about Jews almost as a third party (as Chouraqui speaks of Christians). Still, for Daniélou there is no room for the Jewish witness in contemporary salvation history.[23]

Hans Urs von Balthasar, another Roman Catholic theologian, writing as recently as 1967, speaks of the "reprobation of Israel" as the means by which salvation has been offered to the Gentile world. The relation between Israel and the Church is one of promise and fulfillment, but Jesus, as a Jew, has "roots both in Abraham and in heaven." Nevertheless, theologically speaking, modern Judaism does not have an "historical mission

22. *Idem, The Jews*, pp. 25, 69, 70; Jacob Bernard Agus, "Response to Father Daniélou's *Dialogue with Israel* and Cardinal Bea's *The Church and the Jewish People*," in J. B. Agus, *Dialogue and Tradition: The Challenge of Contemporary Judaeo-Christian Thought* (New York: Abelard-Schuman, 1971), gives an extended critique of Daniélou's position, which he labels "theological anti-semitism."

23. Fellow Catholic Augustin Cardinal Bea seems to concur when he says: "It is true that the Jewish people is no longer the people of God in the sense of an institution for the salvation of mankind." Bea, like Daniélou, would not say that Israel has been rejected but only that her function of preparing for the kingdom of God was "finished with the advent of Christ" (*The Church and the Jewish People*, p. 96).

to fulfill in mankind, different from that of the Church, as is constantly alleged."[24]

For Lutheran scholar *Johannes Aagard*, the options are two—either Jesus of Nazareth fulfilled Old Testament messianic prophecies or he corrupted them. For him, it is simply another way of asking whether or not Jesus was raised from the dead (and thereby installed as Messiah). Of course, Aagard answers that, indeed, Jesus is the Messiah and was installed as such at the resurrection. The Christian Church is the Church of the new covenant, the new people of election, meaning that the Christian Church is the sole eschatological reality: "As Christ represented Israel in such a way that he *was* Israel in its election, the Jews rejected their own election by rejecting Christ." But while the Jews have lost their election, they have not lost God's love—God's love is unchanging, his election is not.[25] In Christ the mission of Israel was fulfilled and the inauguration of the kingdom begun. The Church is the new (and only) Israel. Aagard, in describing the meaning of modern Judaism, makes the distinction between the " 'ethnos' called Israel and the 'laos' called Israel." "After the resurrection . . . the 'laos' is an eschatological reality which cannot be identified with any ethnic group whatsoever." With the resurrection, the ethnic Israel is secularized—the Jews have the same calling as all other nations —to recognize the Messiah of God.[26]

For French Catholic scholar *Kurt Hruby*, Jewish-Christian reflection centers on the notion of election. As for Aagard, the election which Israel was privileged to bear was transferred to Christ, the fulfillment of Israel's election.[27] The chosen people are now those who believe in him and who make up his body. Unlike Aagard, Hruby makes no distinction between election and God's love. Israel retains her special election "according to

24. Hans Urs von Balthasar, *Church and World*, chapter entitled "The Church and Israel," pp. 169, 170, 172f.

25. Cf. also R. L. Lindsey, "Salvation and the Jews," *International Review of Missions* 61 (1972):20-37, for another expression of this same viewpoint.

26. Johannes Aagard, "The Church and the Jews in Eschatology," *Lutheran World* 11 (1964):270-278 (pp. 273-275); on this final point, cf. also George Papademetriou, "Jewish Rite in the Christian Church: Ecumenical Possibility," *Scottish Journal of Theology* 26 (1973):466-487: it is "the responsibility of Christians to build up a theology of Christ-Messiah for Israel" (p. 486).

27. *Ibid.*, p. 275.

the flesh"; Hruby does not expand on the nature of this election anymore than to say Israel possesses it.[28] In the light of his Christology, however, election for contemporary Judaism means only a preparation for Christianity. Thus Hruby's ecclesiology is unmistakably supersessionist.[29]

For Hruby Christ is the fulfillment of the Old Testament messianic prophecies and thus the Church must continue to proclaim him as such to the Jews. To a Jew who accepts Christ as Messiah, Hruby would not apply the word "conversion," in the sense of abandoning something, but in the sense of a fulfillment in full awareness of, and fidelity to, all the authentic values of Judaism.[30]

Hence, Hruby's Christology affirms quite strongly "the universal scope of the message and work of Christ." If Judaism's election is linked to any mission at all, that mission is to serve "the progress of Christianity toward its own fulfillment, the second advent of Christ." As a Christological title expressing this, Hruby refers to Jesus as the "disciple of Moses" in order for Christians to "rediscover the present-day role of Judaism to serve the progress of Christianity through the ages."[31] However undefined this relationship between Church and Synagogue is, Christ's claim is quite ultimate and Judaism's contemporary role in God's plan quite subordinate.[32]

28. This is true of Bea's position also; cf. *The Church and the Jewish People*, p. 96.

29. Kurt Hruby, "Peoplehood in Judaism and Christianity," *Theology Digest* 22 (1974):3-12 (p. 11: "New Testament sources point to the transfer of the people of God concept to the community of the disciples [cites 2 Cor. 6:16]. . . . This new reality of God's people is gradually defined in New Testament writings, and the key term is *ekklesia* in the sense of 'the definite gathering around God of the people he has chosen.' "

30. *Idem*, "Reflections on the Dialogue," pp. 120f, 126f in *Brothers in Hope*, pp. 106-131, edited by John M. Oesterreicher (New York: Herder and Herder, 1970); see also Hruby's "Israël, peuple de Dieu: exist-t-il une théologie d'Israël dans l'Eglise?" *Lumiére et Vie* 18 (1969): 59-82.

31. *Idem*, "Jesus, Disciple of Moses: The True Relationship of Christianity and Judaism" *Encounter Today* 8 (1972):4-10 (pp. 6f).

32. See also K. H. Rengstorf, "The Place of the Jew in the Theology of the Christian Mission," *Lutheran World* 11 (1964):279-295 (pp. 194f): "God wills the existence of the Jews for the sake of the church and its proclamation . . . it is the Jews who shall continue to close themselves off to Jesus whom God is using to keep the memory within Christianity alive that according to its nature it is a messianic community, and nothing else." Quoted by permission.

Common among the Christologies of discontinuity which we have outlined is an emphasis on the unique and universal salvific efficacy of Christ. Each of these Christologies understands Jesus of Nazareth as the perfect fulfillment of Old Testament messianic prophecies. However, this assertion of fulfillment was, in each case, an uncritical one (with Jocz as a possible exception). That is, without delineating the nature of Israel's messianic hopes (see fn. 7 in the previous chapter), sweeping statements that Jesus was their fulfillment were made. In the few cases where Christian thinkers admitted that Jesus was not all that Israel had hoped for, they asserted that Jesus *transformed* messianic expectation and thereby was more than Israel had hoped for. In Christ, Israel's election found its fulfillment and new embodiment—Christ is the new elect of God, and his Church, his body, is the new people of God. The connection between Christology and ecclesiology is quite pronounced here, but it is interesting to note that the justification for the Christian mission to the Jews (almost universal among the theologians of discontinuity) was often grounded, not in the absolute Christological claims, but in the Christian ecclesiological self-understanding: "We Christians cannot give up some kind of mission to the Jews because, if we did, we would no longer be Church." In other words, the missionary exigency flows from the nature of the Church more than from the absolute claims of Christ.[33]

Understandably, theologians of discontinuity find it hard to acknowledge religious significance for contemporary Judaism: although ancient Israel was faithful to the God of the covenant, her mission was completed by, fulfilled by, and transferred to, the Church, the Body of Christ. To guard against any antisemitism which may issue from such a Christological position, these theologians are left only with exhortations to Christian love and the call to respect men and women of all religions. Israel was special because of her mission as preparation for Christ and in the mystery of God's plan. Israel is still the object of God's

33. See, for example, Joseph R. Estes, "Jewish-Christian Dialogue as Mission," p. 9; George A. F. Knight, "Beyond Dialogue," p. 172; cf. also Vatican II's "Decree on the Missionary Activity of the Church," Article 2, p. 585, Abbott, for an official statement on the missionary nature of the Church. But see Jacob Jocz, *Christians and Jews*, p. 47.

love, but, with the absolute coming of the Messiah, Israel has ceased to have positive meaning in salvation history.

Even if these theologians of discontinuity are uncritical in reading of Old Testament prophecies and their fulfillment in Jesus of Nazareth, they do take the historical development of Christology seriously insofar as they do not just write it off to a Hellenizing (and corrupting) decline. Alongside absolute claims for Christ, the theologians describe and encourage a benevolent attitude toward the Jewish people. They are unanimous in deploring disrespectful tactics of proselytizing and often they describe their approach to Jews in dialogue as one of "witness," not of argument or persuasion. In the end, however, they are victims of their own absolutist claims, for they are forced, by their Christology, to imply that Jews are blind to their own Scriptures, whose only proper understanding is a Christological one.

Also, in places, an unnuanced view of biblical election leaves the theologians of discontinuity applying election to the nations of the world (to whom Christ opened the election or covenant), but no longer applying it to present-day children of the Promise. Of late, there has been much scholarly interest in the biblical notions of election, but it is beyond the scope of our book to go into them here. Nevertheless, it can at least be said that "the doctrine that Israel was rejected and the Church chosen to be a new people of God" is simplistic[34]—to say nothing of the biblical notions of "old" and "new" covenants.[35]

34. Nils A. Dahl, "Election and the People of God—Some Comments," p. 36, in *Speaking of God Today*, Opsahl, ed. On the doctrine of election, see also Frank M. Cross, "A Christian Understanding"; Robert E. Cushman, "Biblical Election as Sacred History: A Study in the Ancient History of Ecumenism," in John Deschner *et al.*, eds., *Our Common History as Christians: Essays in Honor of Albert C. Outler*, pp. 179-216 (New York: Oxford University Press, 1975); S. Siegel, "Election and the People of God: A Jewish Perspective," *Lutheran Quarterly* 21 (1969):437-450; Amos Wilder, "The Church and Israel in the Light of the Election," *Studia Evangelica* IV, pp. 347-357, edited by F. M. Cross (Berlin, 1968).

35. See, for example, Leohnard Goppelt, "Israel and the Church in Today's Discussion and in Paul," *Lutheran World* 10 (1963):352-372, who himself must be numbered among the theologians of discontinuity, p. 364: "In what sense . . . is Israel's covenant 'old'? The concepts 'old' and 'new' are not meant to distinguish various epochs of worldly history, but eschatologically to distinguish the old and the new creation." Quoted by permission.

It is around these notions then—of fulfillment, Messiah, election, and covenant—that more recent study on Jewish-Christian relations has focused. The ramifications on, and ultimate foundation in, Christology of these particular doctrines are quite evident and decisive.

2. *Christologies of Continuity*

Another group of Christian biblical scholars and theologians, attempting to profess Christianity while maintaining at the same time the continued validity of Judaism, has begun to articulate a Christology less absolutist (not necessarily relativistic) than the group described above. These theologians of continuity believe that some traditional aspects of Christology must be discarded or understood anew so that a faithful rendering of belief in Jesus Christ might be put forward without, at the same time, crowding out the Jewish witness and validity. These Christian thinkers see Christianity as taking part with (not replacing) the Jews in the People of God. Theology of "continuity" here means that, with the coming of Christ, the election, chosenness, and love of God for Israel were not transferred to the Christian Church, leaving the Jewish people without a God, mission or validity. In other words, theologies of continuity are decidedly non-supersessionist. Theologians of continuity, for the most part, "view the Jewish 'no' to Jesus as a positive contribution to the ultimate salvation of mankind, not as an act of unfaithfulness or haughty blindness."[36]

John T. Pawlikowski, in an article whose concern and method are very similar to those of this paper, sees the Christologies of continuity divided basically between those which "see Judaism and Christianity as two basically distinct religions despite their shared biblical patrimony [and those which believe in] the simultaneous and complementary participation of Christianity and Judaism in the same covenant."[37] These are respec-

36. John T. Pawlikowski, "Christ and the Jewish-Christian Dialogue," p. 2.

37. *Ibid.*, pp. 2, 7.

tively the double and single covenant theories. Almost universal among theologians of either category, however, is the belief that Jesus of Nazareth did not absolutely fulfill the messianic prophecies, and, therefore, for them to call Jesus the Messiah is to redefine the meaning of that term. Without being overly rigorous in our assigning the theologians to either category, we will outline the Christological claims and trends of the theologians of continuity in the Jewish-Christian encounter.

a. *Two-Covenant Theologians*[38]

Theologian *Peter Chirico*, in an attempt to develop a bridge theology between Judaism and Christianity, focuses on a misunderstanding of the nature of revelation which has left Christians with a false understanding of fulfillment. Chirico thinks that Christians cannot relinquish all forms of fulfillment

---

38. The two-covenant theory is most often associated with the early twentieth-century Jewish philosopher Franz Rosenzweig. Almost becoming a Christian, Rosenzweig rather rediscovered his own Judaism and spent much of his life describing the relation in God's plan between Judaism and Christianity. Christians need a God-man, for it is only through such that they can come to the Father; the Jews are already with the Father through the covenant. Christianity is by its nature missionary as Judaism is by its nature destined and commanded to survive. Rootedness in Christianity comes from its spiritual birth into another kingdom; rootedness for the Jew comes from his natural birth, etc. As Nahum Glatzer states, for Rosenzweig "both [Judaism and Christianity] are representations of the real world (and as such equal before God) and spell the end of the heathen view of the world. Judaism, which stands before God, stands in contrast to Christianity, which is sent out to conquer the unredeemed world and is forever marching toward God." Reprinted by permission of Schocken Books, Inc. from the Introduction to *Franz Rosenzweig: His Life and Thought by Mahum N. Glatzer* (Copyright 1953 by Schocken Books, Inc.), p. xxv. See also Eugen Rosenstock-Huessy, *Judaism Despite Christianity: Letters between Eugene Rosenstock-Huessy and Franz Rosenzweig* (Alabama: University of Alabama Press, 1969), esp. pp. 134f; Franz Rosenzweig, *The Star of Redemption*, translated from the 2nd edition of 1930 by William W. Hello (New York: Holt, Rinehart and Winston, 1970), esp. pp. 413-416; Eliezer Berkovits, *Major Themes in Modern Philosophies of Judaism* (New York: KTAV, 1974), pp. 43-46. For critiques of Rosenzweig's two-covenant theory, see Samuel Hugo Berman, "Israel and the *Oikoumenē*," in *Studies in Rationalism, Judaism and Universalism,* pp. 47-66, edited by Raphael Loewe (London: Routledge and Kegan Paul, 1966), esp. pp. 61-63; Markus Barth, *Israel and the Church,* pp. 38f; Maurice G. Bowler, 'Rosenzweig on Judaism and Christianity—The Two Covenant Theory," *Judaism* 22 (1963):475-481.

theology with regard to Christ, but Christians have been the victims of thinking of fulfillment only in terms of *past* fulfillment in Jesus and contemporary fulfillment in the Church. Revelation is a mission rather than an accomplishment:[39]

> Revelation [is] . . . manifested in concrete man himself who is a derived revelation of God to the degree that he images forth Jesus Christ, who, as true man, is the manifestation of God in creation.[40]

There are obvious Rahnerian drifts in Chirico's suggestions —for the Christian believes that whenever messianic prophecies are fulfilled in the present (revelation as mission), Christ is active there whether the bearer of the revelation is conscious of it or not. The Jewish people await the future Messianic times with the Christian people, but Christians claim to know the Messiah's identity before he appears. But until that time, the Christian must respect—and not attempt to convert—other bearers of God's revelation.

Chirico obviously has hit upon an important theme here. In emphasizing the incarnational aspect of revelation, however, he does avoid coming to grips with traditional Christological claims of divinity and the necessity of explicit belief in Jesus of Nazareth as the Christ. This sets up a tension which Chirico acknowledges but does not resolve:

> Christians will never believe that it is ideal that Jews do not recognize Christ any more than they should ever believe that their own living out of Christianity is ideal. But they must come to see . . . that the concrete Jewish community

---

39. Rabbi Jacob Agus has suggested similar notions in two places: in "Revelation as Quest—A Contribution to Ecumenical Thought," *JES* 9 (1972):521-543, where he suggests that the trialogue among Jews, Christians, and Moslems will be aided by thinking of revelation as a quest rather than as an accomplishment; and in "Israel and the Jewish-Christian Dialogue," *JES* 6 (1969):18-36, where he coordinates the Jewish interpretations of the state of Israel with the Christian notions of the kingdom of God, and for both, the kingdom/Israel is to be best understood as a vocation rather than as a fulfillment.

40. Peter Chirico, "Christian and Jew Today," p. 756. Quoted by permission.

manifests aspects of the very revelation of God that they themselves do not manifest.[41]

The same criticisms might be leveled at Chirico that are leveled at Rahner's anonymous Christianity,[42] but it must be said to Rahner's critics as to Chirico's that the theory of the anonymous Christian is not a technique of conversion or of dialogue. It is a way for *Christians* to understand other religions within a Christological view of history, while maintaining the other's validity in itself and not (only) as a preparation for Christianity.

One might also say that Chirico has changed so radically the notion of fulfillment that he, like the theologians of discontinuity, has uncritically transformed this notion without justification for such transformation from the Hebrew Scriptures. But Chirico is careful to make *accomplished* fulfillment a thing of the future and fulfillment as mission a common concern of the present. Christians, no more than Jews, have the obligation of realizing the messianic promises in the present.

Eva Marie Fleischner, professor at Montclair State College, New Jersey, is one scholar who has noted that, in the very shift from a missionary to a dialogic posture with references to the Jews, there are grave Christological, soteriological, and ecclesiological implications. In order to systematize a Christology which allows room for the permanent validity of the Jewish witness, while admitting the perennial tension that must exist between Jews and Christians, Fleischner holds that the multiple Christologies within the New Testament itself allow for, and legitimize, other theological pluralism. Fleischner rejects a Logos-Christology proposed by Rahner as the solution; she sees the application of "implicit Christianity" to Jews as the denying

41. *Ibid.*, p. 761.
42. For criticism of Rahner's notion of anonymous Christianity with regard to the Jews, see Eva Marie Fleischner, *Judaism,* p. 133, and Gregory Baum, "Introduction," pp. 16f. For the only comments on the relation of Judaism to Christianity by Rahner which this writer could locate, see Karl Rahner and F. G. Friedmann, "Unbefangenheit und Anspruch," *Stimmen der Zeit* 173 (1966):81-97; cf. also Karl Rahner, "Christianity and Non-Christian Religions," *Theological Investigations* (Baltimore: Helicon Press, 1966), 5:115-134.

of Jewish freedom and identity, and as imposing on them the Christian vision of truth.[43]

In her dissertation, Fleischner's main concern is the Christian missionary posture vis-à-vis the Jews in German theological writings since 1945, so her Christological proposal is abbreviated and provisional. She abstracts from Matthew's geneology to suggest the use of the Christological title "Jesus, Son of Abraham":

> It is scriptural, yet not worn thin through use; it points to Jesus' 'Jewishness' through his descent from Abraham, Father of the Jewish people; it is not a Messianic title, such as 'Son of David,' hence acceptable to Jews; and it would be difficult for Christians to find any grounds on which to object to it.[44]

Still Fleischner admits that the heart of the Christological difficulty between Jews and Christians

> . . . is not Jesus of Nazareth, Son of Abraham, a Jew among Jews. It is the Christian's claim that in Jesus of Nazareth the Kingdom of God has come among men—the confession of Jesus as the Christ—that is the central issue.[45]

Fleischner does not resolve this difficulty but leaves it in all its baldness and force. She does admit that, on the final day, all peoples will be brought to Christ, but she cautions against " 'using' Judaism as an end for Christianity's perfection." The only solution that would neither compromise Judaism's independent validity nor surrender belief in Christ is "dialogue without reservation." "Dialogue of this kind does not imply a letting go of Christ, but of our ways of conceiving him, our dogmatic formulations, also in the area of Christology."[46] While

---

43. Eva Marie Fleischner, *Judaism*, pp. 134ff, 133.
44. *Ibid.*, p. 125, compare Kurt Hruby's suggestion that Jesus be referred to as "Jesus, Disciple of Moses." Quoted by permission.
45. *Ibid.*, p. 129, Quoted by permission.
46. *Ibid.*, pp. 141, 143.

calling for such dialogue, Fleischner does not suggest where it will go—only that the parties involved be open to following it to its conclusion.

For *James Parkes*, pioneering Anglican theologian in Jewish-Christian relations, Judaism and Christianity offer different yet complementary aspects of the one revelatory plan of God. This revelation of God speaks to the perennial tension in man between community and the individual:

> The destiny of what we must now call 'the Gentile Church' is equally determined by the revelation on which it rests: the ultimate value of man as person 'for whom Christ dies.' . . . It is the power of the risen Christ to make new men of 'Jew and Greek, bound and free.' . . . That divine power, which came to its full expression in the Incarnation, it rightly traces back through history, wherever it sees men as persons accepting the will of God and being changed thereby.

> The distinction between the two revelations [Judaism and Christianity] . . . lies in the complementary, not contradictory, sphere of the individual. That highest purpose of God which Sinai reveals to men in community, Calvary reveals to man as an end in himself.[47]

Parkes, in his Christology, stresses the aspects of atonement and sacrifice—notions which he thinks Christians have downplayed or ignored in more modern Christologies. The message and effects of Christ's sacrifice on the cross are of univer-

---

47. James Parkes, *The Foundations of Judaism and Christianity* (Chicago: Quadrangle Books, 1960), p. 132; *idem, Judaism and Christianity* (London: Victor Gallancz, Ltd., 1948), p. 30. This breakdown of the mutually valid and complementary revelations of Judaism and Christianity are the objective correspondents to the interior dispositions Martin Buber calls the two kinds of faith, "emunah" and "pistis": "An Israel striving after the renewal of its faith through the rebirth of the person and a Christianity striving for the renewal of its faith through the rebirth of nations would have something as yet unsaid to say to each other and a help to give to one another—hardly to be conceived at this time": Martin Buber, *Two Kinds of Faith* (London: Routledge and Kegan, Paul, Ltd., 1951), p. 174.

sal application—the revelation to man as individual and as an end in himself. To men in community and to men as individuals, Jews and Christians are equal, complementary partners in bringing mankind to the messianic age, each making his own proper contribution based on the revelation from which each respectively springs.

Parkes views the Christocentric preoccupation of the Church as an unfortunate development, which development has led to "deplorable beliefs and activities," such as the belief of salvation only through Christ.[48] Rather, the Church should reformulate its doctrine of the Trinity:

> If we use the word 'channel' in place of person [in formulating the doctrine of the Trinity], I believe that power flows from one unknowable godhead through three equal channels, and that each channel reached its fullness at an appropriate moment in the history of creation. I believe that the first such moment was at Sinai. The second was at the Incarnation. Consequently I hold the right relations between Judaism and Christianity to be a creative tension within a single trinitarian theology. Just as man as social being lives in perpetual tension with himself as person, so the power which flows through the channel of the Incarnation is in tension, creative or destructive, with the power that flows from Sinai.[49]

Many Christians have noted the difficulty of the Trinitarian doctrine in the Jewish-Christian dialogue, but only Parkes has suggested that it may provide the answer to the clash between religions. Parks holds that the tension between the faiths is intended by God, but if each faith would grant to the other the necessity and value of the other's revelation

48. According to Parkes, this began in Paul's letters, as John T. Pawlikowski, "The Church and Judaism: The Thought of James Parkes," *JES* 6 (1969):573-597, comments (p. 594): Paul's "basic failure was to produce a permanent Judaeo-Christian Church which would embody the teachings of Jesus and yet not divorce itself completely from Judaism. Parkes attributes this failure primarily to Paul's concentration on and mystical absorption in the Messiah." Quoted by permission.

49. Reprinted by permission of Schocken Books, Inc. from *Prelude to Dialogue* by James Parkes (Copyright 1969 by James Parkes), p. 200.

through Sinai and Calvary, then each would come to discover the creative quality of their mutual tension.

Since both Judaism and Christianity have complementary roles in God's one revelatory plan, then their missions are necessarily complementary as well—to witness to the world that God elects man as nation (as exemplified in Israel) and as individual (as exemplified in Christianity). Thus the doctrine of election assumes the characteristic of complementarity as well.[50] Parkes does not deal with the Christian claim that Jesus is the Messiah other than to say that Christocentrism was a later shift from the original teachings of Jesus which were thoroughly Jewish in character.[51] Parkes claims—repeatedly—that he is orthodox in his Christological views, yet he leaves the assertion of the Messiahship of Jesus quite vague, noting only that Judaism looked forward more to a messianic age than to a personal Messiah. This same sort of Christian transformation of a Jewish idea happened to the notion of covenant as well.[52]

Thus James Parkes maintains within the very tensions, which he thinks are divinely intended, that Jesus is divine, that he is Messiah, that Judaism and Christianity are complementary expressions of the one revelatory plan of God, that the Trinity is the key to understanding this complementarity, and that both Christianity and Judaism are elect of God.

The two-covenant theory has obviously been worked out in different ways by different people, but, for the most part, those who endorse a second covenant find its beginning in Jesus of Nazareth. *J. Coert Rylaarsdam*, however, finds the evidence of two covenants within the Hebrew Scriptures themselves: the covenant with Israel and the covenant with David. The mission of the Jews after Jesus Christ, using the Exodus as the objective moment of revelation and carrying on the covenant with Israel, is to proclaim and further the coming of the final day of

---

50. This theme of complementarity is frequent among theologies of continuity—and is denied by theologians of discontinuity. For examples of theories of complementarity variously worked out, see Frank M. Cross, Jr., "A Christian Understanding of the Election of Israel," p. 85; Martin Buber, *Two Types*; Monika Hellwig, "Proposal," pp. 181ff; *et al.*
51. James Parkes, "Judaism and the Jewish People."
52. *Idem, Prelude to Dialogue*, pp. 55, 38.

triumph in history: "For Jewish faith, social and ethical responsibility is a direct corollary of its witness that time and history
are the scene and means of God's redemption."[53]

The problem of Christology which divides Judaism and
Christianity lies precisely in locating the day of triumph: "The
dilemmas of Christology today are mostly the dilemmas of history and eschatology. If Christianity is an eschatological faith,
how can it be an historical faith as well?"[54] Rylaarsdam claims
that, however Jesus understood himself, his followers soon after
interpreted his career as an eschatological event. It is only in
recent years that Christians have become more concerned about
the history of Jesus and the historical realization of the messianic age. The New Testament, from which Christians are
seeking such a history, is itself the expression of an eschatological interpretation of the Hebrew Scriptures.

But as Rylaarsdam points out, the paradox of an eschatological understanding of the day of triumph is already present in
the Hebrew Scriptures in the covenant with David. And it is this
covenant which the New Testament takes over and expands. If
the covenant with Israel had been employed to understand
Jesus, with its salvation-history view of seeing God's acting in
visible historical events, Jesus would have been interpreted as
God acting once again, but not uniquely, finally, or as Messiah
—and certainly not as God-man. Among the features found in
the covenant of confederacy (= the covenant with Israel) but
lacking in the Davidic covenant were renewal ceremonies, the
particularity of Israel's election, communalism (in contradistinction to individualism), and emphasis on the historical (in
contradistinction to the cosmic, the world of the non-human
contingent), the ongoing sequence of promise-fulfillment (in
contradistinction to remembering—thereby to make present—
the primordial and absolute); in summary:

[The differences between the two covenants are] the abso-

---

53. J. Coert Rylaarsdam, "Common Ground and Difference," *Journal of
Religion* 43 (1963):261-270. Quoted by permission.

54. *Idem*, "Jewish-Christian Relationship: The Two-Covenants and the
Dilemmas of Christology," *JES* 9 (1972):249-270 (p. 250); see footnote on p.
250 of his article for his careful definitions of history and eschatology.

lute and primordial over against the contingent and historical; the orientation to the past versus the orientation to the
future; and a decreed divine determinism in tension with
assumptions of human freedom and responsibility. . . .
What made this new faith [Christianity] distinctive from
the faith of Israel, which had also combined them [the two
covenants], was that it reversed the order of priority as-
signed to the covenants. Whereas in Israel the Covenant of
David is made subservient to the Covenant of the Confederacy, in Christianity the opposite is the case.[55]

It is important to note, therefore, that the two covenants of
which Rylaarsdam speaks are not two placed one after another,
but rather two that are found both in the Hebrew Scriptures
and in the New Testament. Any notion of the Hebrew Scriptures as only preparation for the New is cancelled, and each of
the testaments acts as a reminder to the other of the forgotten
elements emphasized in their respective covenant.

While he does not present a reformulated Christology, Rylaarsdam does provide a direction that would insure the mutual
validity and interdependence of the two religions. Rylaarsdam
does not suggest that Jesus is not the Messiah or that he is not
divine—he describes how Christians, inspired by the Davidic
covenant, understandably interpreted him that way.

Gregory Baum is less chary to suggest some of the directions a Christological reformulation might take, but even he
presents not so much a revised Christological belief as a set of
conditions within which such reformulation might take place.

55. *Ibid.*, p. 262; these distinctions are reminiscent of what Rosemary
Ruether calls the "spiritualizing of the eschatological . . . historicizing of the
eschatological" (Rosemary Ruether, "Theological Anti-Semitism in the New
Testament," *The Christian Century* 85 [1968]: 191-196 [p. 194]). Monika Hellwig, "Proposal," thinks that Karl Rahner asserts essentially the same thing on
phenomenological rather than scriptural ground in his essay, "The Hermeneutics of Eschatological Assertions," *Theological Investigations*, IV:323-346 (Baltimore: Helicon Press, 1966). Interestingly, Ruether does not cite Rylaarsdam's
article in her book (*Faith and Fratricide*) although Gregory Baum, in his introduction, does (p. 10). Much of the edge of Ruether's criticism would be taken
away if Rylaarsdam's suggestion is true, that is, if even within the Hebrew
Scriptures there is a trend toward historicizing and spiritualizing the eschatological.

Although one might surmise that Baum's Christology is the same as that formulated by Rosemary Ruether, a careful reading of that introduction indicates some points of Christological divergence and an unqualified approval of only her method of investigation.[56]

For the sake of conciseness, we put in point-form what Baum considers to be the conditions for a Christian formulation of Christology in the face of the Jewish-Christian encounter. If, after Auschwitz, the preaching of the Christian message is to be freed from the implied negation of Jewish existence, then:

1. the Church must not consider itself as successor of Israel, substituting for the original, but now obsolete people of God;

2. the Church must acknowledge the abiding validity of Judaism, not as preparation for Christianity, but in itself;

3. the Church must recognize that its own Christological reading of the ancient Scriptures does not exhaust their meaning but leaves room for a synagogal reading;

4. the Church must reinterpret the claim that Jesus is the one mediator without whom there is no salvation;

5. the Church cannot be satisfied with a Logos-Christology that presents Jews simply as anonymous Christians;[57]

6. the Church ought to understand the 'absolute and universal significance' of Jesus not as invalidating other religions

56. This may or may not be the case. A. Roy Eckardt ("Comments at Israel Study Group Meeting, April 5, 1975, on Rosemary Ruether's FAITH AND FRATRICIDE" [xerox]) thinks that there is a "basic inconsistency between the viewpoint of the major author and that of Gregory Baum in his Introduction to the volume. Baum affirms what he calls the 'aspect of absolute and universal significance' respecting Jesus (p. 15). The problem is that through his absolutist Christology in the context of the end of time (p. 17), Baum preserves the traditional Christian ideology that it is through Jesus Christ that the Jews will ultimately be saved. Ruether denies this."

57. *Idem*; see "Introduction," pp. 16-17; "The Jews, Faith and Ideology," *The Ecumenist* 10 (1971-72): 71-76 (pp. 75f); but see his earlier article, "The Doctrinal Basis," p. 239, where he affirms, "What God has done for men in Jesus Christ is universal and irrevocable. . . . This mystery is announced, believed and visibly celebrated in the Church. But this same mystery is at work everywhere in a hidden way. . . . Because of Christ's universal mediation, the redemptive realities revealed in the Scriptures, such as repentance, justification by faith, conversion and grace, are present everywhere in human life. God in Jesus Christ is at work in the entire human race."

but as offering a critique applicable to all religions, including the Christian one;[58]

7. the Church should proclaim Jesus, not as the one who has already fulfilled all the promises, but as the pivotal point of history, the guarantee of God's final victory, and the bringer of redemption in the full and final sense only at the end of time;

8. the Church should proclaim the redemption present in Jesus now as unfulfilled messianism, as divine grace empowering believers to pray and struggle that God's will be done on earth and to yearn for the final coming of the kingdom.[59]

Thus Baum is among those who speak of fulfillment eschatologically. Jesus is Christ in the fullest sense only at the end of time. Jesus was Messiah in a proleptic, anticipatory way; Jesus brings the grace that makes humanity yearn for fulfillment; Jesus reveals the passage from humiliation to elevation; but the sentence that Jesus is the Christ will be true in the fullest sense only at the end of time—this, Baum thinks, secures the abiding religious validity of Judaism. Although this solves the present problem of making theological room for Judaism, one wonders whether this might only be putting the question one step back. That is, how different is it, substantially, to say (a) that the Jews are not called upon now to recognize Jesus as Messiah (either historically fulfilled or eschatologically proleptic), (b) that he is working in them unrecognized, or (c) that in the end time all will be reconciled in Christ. The Christian faith has traditionally claimed that Christ is the first-born of the new creation (to be radically established only in the end time) but also that Jesus Christ is the second person of the Trinity. Baum does not speak to this second area of traditional Christology. Further, one wonders whether Judaism is any less preparatory in the theologies, such as Baum's, which place the inevitability of acknowledging Christ not in the present but in the undefined future. Jewish scholar Manfred Vogel comments on this modern trend

58. Gregory Baum, "Introduction," p. 15.
59. *Idem*, "Introduction," pp. 17f; see also H. Berkhof, "Israel as a Theological Problem," pp. 341f; Markus Barth, *Israel and the Church*, p. 22; Krister Stendahl, "Judaism and Christianity: Then and Now," pp. 112ff, in *Death of Dialogue and Beyond*, edited by Sanford Seltzer and Max L. Stackhouse.

to put the resolution of Jewish-Christian tensions in the end times:

> We can perhaps also understand why Christian theologians who want to let the problem of the Jewish non-acceptance of Jesus rest . . . resort to the theological scheme of the *Zwischenzeit* and the second coming. . . . [This] deferment of the problem from the present to the future . . . [enables] one to overcome the urgency of the present and accept the *status quo* for the time being. . . . [This] means that the messianic claim of Jesus vis-à-vis the Jewish people is cancelled for the present. If the first coming of Jesus makes a messianic claim on the world, the Jews are exempt! . . . Thus the Christian can overcome the disquietude caused by Jewish non-acceptance of Jesus only by surrendering for the time being the messianic claim.[60]

It may be asking too much of Baum to cover all the Christological bases in his few schematic essays on the subject. Although he has written on, and been concerned with, the Jewish-Christian encounter for many years, his focus on Christology has been only more recent. Nevertheless, of all the authors cited here, Baum has asked in the most fundamental and incisive way the very question this thesis has repeatedly raised. He has suggested and negated certain avenues of solution, himself finding most sympathy with the position of Rosemary Ruether.

Rosemary Radford Ruether, probably the most radical of the Christians in the Jewish-Christian dialogue, claims that the Christological hermeneutic of the New Testament writers is based on a twofold interpretation of the Old Testament as positive prophetic texts fulfilled and/or transformed by Jesus and negative texts of the faithless nation fulfilled by the Jewish people.[61]

With regard to the first, Jesus as Messiah, Ruether shows how Christians could have understood Jesus as fulfilling the

---

60. Manfred Vogel, "The Problem of Dialogue between Judaism and Christianity," *JES* 4 (1967):684-699 (p. 689, fn. 2). Quoted by permission.
61. See Rosemary Ruether, *Faith and Fratricide*, pp. 65, 72, 112, 116, 160.

prophecies only by a twofold process of historicizing the eschatological (primarily Luke, who, in the absence of Christ's return, interpreted the Church as the beginning of the kingdom's
establishment, superseding the old Chosen People) and spiritualizing the eschatological (primarily John and Paul, who made
the eschatological events of the messianic era a matter of inter-
nal, undetectable transformations rather than observable events
in an undefined future).[62] Both these developments Ruether
credits to the non-appearance of Christ in messianic victory
after the resurrection event, thus necessitating this radical reun-
derstanding of the Hebrew messianic prophecies and their fulfillment in Jesus.[63] Ruether sees this recasting of Hebrew notions of prophecy and fulfillment as essentially flawed and
illegitimate, especially since this recasting results in the attribu-
tion of absolute finality in Jesus as the only way to God. This
result, Ruether claims, is anti-Judaic and is the theological basis
for the sad history of Christian antisemitism. In a sentence,
Ruether suggests that "the messianic meaning of Jesus' life,
then, is paradigmatic and proleptic in nature, not final and fulfilled."[64] We will return below to this positive solution which
Ruether proposes.

The second development, the negative texts of the Hebrew
Scriptures applied to the Jewish people, had just as devastating
effects as the first. Ruether illustrates how early Christian writers, starting with the evangelists themselves, used Jewish terms
to validate and explain its separation from Judaism. That is,
Christian writers, to bolster and support their position vis-à-vis
Judaism, while trying to explain why the Jews did not recognize
and accept Jesus as Messiah, selected Old Testament prophecies

62. Jürgen Moltmann (*The Crucified God* [New York: Harper & Row,
1974], p. 101) questions whether Christians ever really believed in such an "in-
teriorization of salvation": "Even for Christians, Jesus, the crucified, cannot be
understood without suffering for the unredeemed condition of the world, or
without the hope of the kingdom which he has revealed to all the godless. In
view of the misery of the creation, the fact that the atonement is already accomplished, although its struggle continues, is incomprehensible without the future of the redemption of the body and of the peace which brings the struggle to
an end." Quoted by permission.

63. Rosemary Ruether, "Theological Anti-Semitism," pp. 194f; *Faith and
Fratricide*, p. 248.

64. *Idem, Faith and Fratricide*, p. 249.

about blindness, reprobation, and infidelity and applied them to the Jews to show that the Jews' infidelity had been foretold even in their own scriptures. This exegetical effort Ruether calls "the left-hand of Christology," and it forms the basis of the *Adversus Judaeos* tradition which Ruether so amply delineates.[65]

Thus the foundation of Ruether's critique lies on the illegitimate interpretation of promise and fulfillment, positively applied to Jesus as Messiah and final revelation and negatively applied to the Jews as a blind, reprobate, abandoned people of God. This interpretation has had its social expression in antisemitism, with its logical, if not inevitable, conclusion in the holocaust. The only solution for this situation is a radical reinterpretation and recasting of the Church's Christological belief, starting with the affirmation of the abiding validity of the Jewish religious expression—which affirmation admittedly relativizes Christ's position. Ruether only sketches her positive Christological proposal in her *Faith and Fratricide*, a work which Baum admits is primarily a negative critique of the "ideological deformation of the Christian religion."[66] Nevertheless the necessary relativizing of Christ's role which Ruether suggests consists of viewing the messianic work of Jesus as proleptic and paradigmatic:

> This paradigmatic and proleptic view of the messianic work of Jesus is the only theologically and historically valid way of interpreting it consistent with biblical faith and historical realism. . . . Messianic absolutism . . . generated Christian totalitarianism and imperialism. . . . [Only] by reading the Resurrection in a paradigmatic and proleptic way can the Church avoid making the absolutistic claims about itself which are belied by its own history. . . .

> Before it was anything else, the Christian messianic experience in Jesus was a Jewish experience created out of Jewish hope. As an experience of messianic ecstasy, born of the

65. *Ibid.*, pp. 64-182.
66. Gregory Baum, "Introduction," p. 18.

dream of biblical faith, it becomes paradigmatic and foundational for reaffirming this hope in the final coming of God's Kingdom that is definitive for the heirs of that community which experienced it. But others remember this history quite differently.[67]

How such an understanding might function, Ruether illustrates by paralleling the Christian's experience of the Resurrection with the Jewish experience of the Exodus:

The story of Jesus parallels, it does not negate, the Exodus. It is another story, born from Abraham's promise, which becomes the paradigm of salvation for Christians. In each case, the experience of salvation in the past is recounted as the paradigm for continued hope experienced in the present and pointing to that final hope which is still ahead of both Jews and Christians. When Easter is seen, not as superseding and fulfilling the Exodus, but as reduplicating it, then the Christian can affirm his faith through Jesus in a way that no longer threatens to rob the Jew of his past, eliminate his future and surround his present existence with rivalrous animosity.[68]

Ruether's positive Christological proposal is worked out in a fascinating, as-yet-unpublished work entitled *Messiah of Israel and the Cosmic Christ: A Study of the Development of Christology in Judaism and Early Christianity.* Fortunately the conclusion to her study, with her creative Christological sugges-

---

67. Rosemary Ruether, *Faith and Fratricide*, pp. 250, 256.
68. *Ibid.*, p. 256. Some of Ruether's tendency to exaggerate or polemicize is apparent here. As has been seen repeatedly on previous pages, Christians do not suggest that the story of Jesus "negates" the Exodus story. Also, one wonders whether Jews would be willing to say that the story of Jesus reduplicates the Exodus event. Further, one wonders whether Jews would settle for only a paradigmatic function of the Exodus in their religious consciousness. By the same token, Christians have traditionally claimed more than a paradigmatic function of the resurrection—that is, that something absolutely unique happened in Jesus. Can a Jew accept that in the same way (or at all) as a Christian can accept that God's liberating power was manifest in Exodus, not only for the Jews, but for Christians themselves?

tion, has been published in a recent issue of *The Ecumenist*.[69]

The first part of Ruether's study outlines the Jewish messianic hopes. Focusing primarily on notions of sacral kingship
(as found in neighboring regions as well as in Israel) and of
Messiah (as found in prophetic literature and Jewish apocalyptic), Ruether situates Jesus as Messiah within these notions, ac-
commodating also other contemporary messianic movements.
Jesus' own self-consciousness is to be understood in the context
of these many influences—that is, Jesus', and contemporary
Jewish, messianic understanding and fulfillment could not be
but political, revolutionary, and recognizable within history. It
was the bias of the New Testament writers which "suppressed
the confrontationist content of Messianic faith and spiritualized
and depoliticized its purpose."[70]

The product of this movement, essentially Jewish in its initial driving force and categories, undertook further transformation in its encounter with Hellenism and Hellenistic Judaism.
This process Ruether describes in terms similar to those of her
former article (cf. fn. 55 in this chapter): de-eschatologizing and
de-politicizing of Messianism in the Synoptics, the interioriza-
tion of resurrection-experience in Paul, and the spiritualizing of
eschatology in John; in a sentence, the historico-cultural development in theology after Jesus was that a Jewish messianic
movement was de-politicized to a universal religion.[71] The gen-
ius of Christianity is that it brings two forms of speculation
together in a new and unique synthesis: God-Anthropos as Ar-
chetypal Man projected back as a cosmogony (a combination of
Gnosticism, Hermeticism, and Hellenistic theology), which Jewish Messianism then projects to a transcendent future:

The roles originally associated with the title 'Messiah' in
the Jewish apocalyptic tradition, such as Eschatological
Judge, Raiser of the dead, apocalyptic Warrior and King
of the Future Age were divorced from Jesus' historical career and placed again in the future, rather than being seen

69. "An Invitation to Jewish-Christian Dialogue: In What Sense Can We
Say That Jesus Was 'The Christ'?" *The Ecumenist*, 10 (1972):17-24.
70. *Idem, Messiah of Israel*, p. 162.
71. *Ibid.*, p. 257; cf. also pp. 288, 299.

as proleptically beginning in his life and death. It was dogmatically believed that it would be he that would return to exercise these future messianic roles, but they ceased to be seen as beginning in his actual historical career, even in a 'hidden' form. So the paradox of Christian Christology, vis-à-vis its Jewish background is that the prime title for Jesus continued to be Christ (Messiah), yet his actual historical role came to be seen in terms of functions which were pre- or non-messianic. The Jewish title 'Messiah,' therefore, differs from the Christian title 'Christ' precisely because the paradox whereby the title 'Christ' must needs be expanded to cover a host of roles within history which were not originally associated with the Messiah, and the primary meaning of Messiah as 'King of the Age to Come' faded from the centre of attention. Finally, both these historical, mediating roles and the ultimate eschatological roles then became absorbed into a cosmological doctrine whereby Jesus could be understood as the Revealer and the Messiah to come because he was the original principle through which God manifested himself to man and through which the world was created. Eschatology was refounded upon transcendent cosmology.[72]

This creative syncretism which had transformed the Jewish notion of messianism, and which had incorporated other non-Jewish religious ideas, could only be rejected by the Jews. To remain faithful to their faith, the Jews could only say "no" to this synthesis of "Jewish, Oriental and Greek myths and philosophies."[73]

In her positive Christological proposal, Ruether hopes to incorporate the Jewish negative judgment on Jesus' messiahship. Rejecting Bultmann's, Pannenberg's and Moltmann's Christologies, Ruether suggests that it is most proper to say that Jesus is *not yet* the Christ. She eschews, however, a theology of progress, a theology of Jesus as the "paradigm of 'perfect men' " (for this abolishes Jesus' finitude and mistakes). Rather:

72. *Ibid.*, p. 314; cf. also pp. 278-280. Quoted by permission.
73. *Idem*, "An Invitation to Jewish-Christian Dialogue," p. 19.

[Jesus is the one] who reveals to us the structure of human existence as it stands in that point of tension between what is and what ought to be. . . . Jesus is our paradigm of hoping . . . and Christ stands as the symbol of the fulfillment of that hope. Jesus Christ, then, stands for that unification of man with his destiny which has still not come, but in whose light we continue to hope and struggle.[74]

Further, while evil still holds its sway, Jesus' coming has made its status an illegitimate one; the world is claimed as God's even while alienated from him. Jesus is the paradigm of hoping, providing, at the same time, firm foundation for the ultimate overthrow of evil and the establishment of God's reign. Jesus is the "archetype for us, of aspiring man who, in readying for the Kingdom, lays claim to this present earth in such a way that the evil powers are already conquered in principle."[75] For the Jews, the story of Exodus functions in the same way, and so they do not need the story of Jesus to locate "hoping man." For Christians, the resurrection is the vindication of the hoping man and the proleptic preview of their own fulfillment. Belief in Jesus as the Christ provides strength for the present struggle.

In this suggestion of a non-ideological and non-imperialistic Christology, Ruether takes very seriously the abiding validity and truth of the Jewish mission and faith. The resurrection and Christ-experience function in a paradigmatic way for Christians in the same way as Exodus functions as a foundation for hope for the Jewish people. Neither invalidates the other; each simply speaks to a different group of people.

Ruether's suggestion is undoubtedly a radical one. She speaks little of the traditional Christological claim of divinity; she speaks seldom of "the resurrection," preferring to speak of "the experience of the resurrection" and the "revelation of the resurrection"—both of which are examples of her spiritualizing the eschatological at the expense of the historical. In this she may be closer to Bultmann whom she criticizes. In some places, the reader might infer that development after Jesus was corrup-

74. *Ibid.*, p. 22. Quoted by permission.
75. *Ibid.*

tive (cf. "An Invitation," p. 19) whereas, in other places, she says that Christianity had brilliant insight to evolve into its new, unique synthesis. Perhaps the most radical revision which Ruether suggests is Christ as the "paradigm of hoping." Traditional Christology has claimed some sort of efficacious quality to Jesus' life, whose life definitively revealed the Father and brought salvation, and through whose life men and women have the possibility of resurrection, forgiveness, and life. For many, "paradigm" may be claiming too little.[76]

We have spent much time on Rosemary Ruether's critique of traditional Christology and on her proposal for a new formulation. This has been done for two reasons: first, because her thought illustrates most vividly the process described in this thesis (that is, in dialogue with the Jewish faith, and in acknowledging the abiding validity of the Jewish religion, one describes his/her faith in Jesus differently), and, second, because her Christological proposal is the most elaborate and detailed of any of the Christian thinkers cited. We further believe that it is her work in this area which will provoke more focused attention to the issue of Christology in the Jewish-Christian dialogue.

John T. Pawlikowski, who has written as much about the Christologies of other scholars as he has suggested one of his own, starts his proposal from the commonly agreed upon foundation of the non-fulfillment by Jesus of Jewish messianic hopes and prophecies. Claiming that the mission of authentic Christianity is to "explicate the uniqueness and mystery of the Christ event," Pawlikowski nevertheless suggests that there is a hitherto little-discussed closeness between Christianity and the Pharisaic revolution within Judaism of the Second Temple period.[77] Pawlikowski enumerates many features of this revolution within Judaism (e.g., speaking with new intimacy of the God-man rela-

76. Indeed, Alan Davies, *Antisemitism*, p. 168, thinks Rosemary Ruether "dissolves Christianity into Judaism when she apparently denies any past historical fulfillment of a once-and-for-all character as far as the Christological faith of the Church is concerned." Davies now thinks this is an unfair criticism of Ruether and wishes he had not made it. Others, though, think that Ruether has diluted the Christian message so much that it has lost all distinctiveness whatsoever.

77. John T. Pawlikowski, "Christ and the Jewish-Christian Dialogue," p. 10.

tion, heightened evaluation of the human person, the resurrection of the dead, etc.). He thinks that "an understanding of the
Pharisaic basis of Christology may make passage of the gulf
[between Judaism and Christianity] at some future date at least
thinkable."[78] Thus Pawlikowski locates the ministry of Jesus
within Pharisaical Judaism whose main focus of ministry was
"emphasizing the utter dignity of each individual person."[79]
Jesus emphasized more than his contemporaries, however, the
worth and rights of the individual.

After Jesus died, and in the wake of the resurrection experience, Christians used the most accessible categories to describe Jesus, that is, Jewish messianic titles. Since historically
recognizable evidence of the Messianic times did not emerge,
the Christian community reinterpreted and transformed the original categories from historical to interior, mystical correspondents. Pawlikowski evaluates this development positively.
The Christological/soteriological implications Pawlikowski expresses as follows:

> Through the ministry and person of Jesus man came to see
> clearly for the first time that humanity is an integral part
> of God. This means that each human person is divine, that
> he or she somehow shares in the constitutive nature of
> God. Christ is the theological symbol the Church has cho-
> sen to express this reality. As we learn from the latter stra-
> ta of the New Testament materials, this humanity has ex-
> isted in the God-head from the very beginning. So in a very
> real sense God did not become man in Jesus. That is the ul-
> timate meaning of the infancy narratives' notion of the Vir-
> gin Birth. God always was man. The Christ Event was
> merely the occasion through which this reality became
> clearly manifest to the world.[80]

And so, in one sense, Pawlikowski acknowledges that
Christ is fulfillment—not of messianic prophecies, but the "fulfillment of the growing sense of the dignity and uniqueness of

78. *Ibid.*, p. 14.
79. *Ibid.*
80. *Ibid.*, pp. 17f. Quoted by permission.

the human person."[81] The mission of the Jewish people is to witness to the other side of man's fulfillment, life in community, peoplehood. That men and women are saved in community is a message of which Christianity must constantly remind itself so that it will not deteriorate into a radical individualism. Furthermore the Jewish concern with history should be an abiding corrective to any Christian temptation to abandon the responsibility of being a co-creator of the world in anticipation of a spiritual kingdom after death.

Pawlikowski's proposal of mutually enhancing and corrective covenants is very reminiscent of Buber's description of the two kinds of faith.[82] What is distinctive about Pawlikowski's suggestion, however, is his grounding his proposal not in notions of faith or covenant, but in the history of pharisaism and the development of Christology in the first few centuries. Pawlikowski, like Ruether, has emphasized the role of Christ as revealer without describing how Christ might be savior or in what way Christians can understand the resurrection. The question, "Has some/everything changed because and since Jesus died and rose?)" is not addressed by Pawlikowski. Yet it is clear that in the traditional Christian answer to this question a certain finality of Christ is found.

b. *Single-Covenant Christologies*

Monika Hellwig, prominent Roman Catholic theologian at Georgetown University, believes that both Judaism and Christianity are charged with complementary roles within the one covenant of God with his people. With those of the two-covenant school, she shares the opinion that it is inaccurate to say Jesus fulfilled the Jewish messianic prophecies; however, false messianic expectations are only ancillary to a neglected or misunderstood notion of the covenant in the Hebrew Scriptures. Christians have emphasized the messianic theme in the Old Testament at the expense of the covenant theme.

81. *Ibid.*, p. 19.
82. See fn. 47 in this chapter.

Like Ruether, Hellwig sees the Christians' absolutizing of Christ to be located in spiritualizing and historicizing the eschatological which has been embodied in the person of Jesus. Rather Jesus' function is that, through him, the Gentiles come to worship the one true God. Messiahship is to be understood as a mission for the entire Church of God (Christians and Jews) to realize in history, not as already realized in Jesus. The complementary character of this mission of the one Church, Hellwig describes as follows:

> The believing Jew of today participates by virtue of his own religious tradition in the universal Church of God, because he orients his life by belief in Christ who is to come, though he does not concretely identify the Christ with the returning Jesus of Nazareth. . . . His faith is complementary with Christian faith as two aspects of the same reality, two historical approaches to the same eschatological fulfillment, two dimensions of mankind's relationship to God.[83]

Thus the Jews witness in a special way to the transcendence and unity of God. Election is a way of saying that God talks first, so Christians are elect by becoming part of the chosen people through Jesus. Jewish election finds its meaning in the messianic meaning that is yet to come. The covenant after Jesus is new only in the sense that now it includes all people.[84]

The practical result which Hellwig sees from such insights is a humbler language about Christian belief in Jesus Christ. Rather than looking to the past for fulfillment of messianic expectations, Christians will look to the future, in the light of the resurrection experience, and they will "expect to be able to recognize Jesus as the heart or core" of eschatological fulfillment. Further, Christians, while not doubting the claim of Jesus' di-

---

83. Monika Hellwig, "Proposal," p. 181; see also pp. 175f, 190f. On the complementary character of Judaism and Christianity, see her article, "Christian Theology," pp. 44, 49. Quoted by permission.

84. *Ibid.*, pp. 190-194; on the meaning of "new covenant," cf. her article, "Christian Theology," pp. 44, 45, 48f; for a similar view about Jesus opening the divine purpose to the whole world, cf. Roland de Corneille, *Christians and Jews: The Tragic Past, and the Hopeful Future* (Toronto: Longmans Canada, Ltd., 1966), pp. 72f.

vinity, should reflect carefully on what such a claim might mean.[85]

Rather than "Jesus is Messiah," Hellwig suggests a "more cautious formulation" of Christological belief in the early Christian prophetic assertion "Jesus is Lord and Christ"; by this assertion, "Christians have pledged themselves to a task of salvation yet to be accomplished."[86] Respecting and recalling the peculiar nature of religious language, especially the analogous use of language, Hellwig suggests that it may be more accurate (than to say Jesus is divine) to assert, in phenomenological terms, "Jesus is the place of encounter of man with the transcendent God, which Christians have experienced as central in all human existence."[87] Claims of salvation only through Jesus found in the New Testament are expressions of kerygmatic urgency produced in, and making sense only from, a background of imminent eschatological expectation. Thus, revelation is not a deposit of propositions about Jesus, but the unformulated speaking of God in the depth of the human heart which finds expression in man's religious traditions.[88] Christians must look then to God's revelation in contemporary Jewish experience to see what God is saying of himself, just as God reveals himself in the experience of the Church.

A. Roy Eckardt, affirming with Hellwig that the significance of Jesus lies in his opening salvation to the Gentiles, nevertheless thinks that messianic fulfillment occurred in Jesus to the extent, and in the sense, that by opening salvation to the Gentiles

. . . a special and essential evil has already been overcome: the hopelessness and loneliness of those who were

85. *Idem,* "Why We Still Can't Talk," pp. 30f; cf. also her article, "Christian Theology," p. 39.

86. *Idem,* "Christian Theology," p. 49.

87. *Ibid.,* p. 50; this notion Hellwig credits to Edward Schillebeeckx.

88. *Ibid.,* p. 51; locating the issue in one's understanding of revelation is very similar to Peter Chirico's proposal outlined above. One might observe here that the function of revelation as critique of one's formulations in addition to its expressive function has been neglected by Hellwig. Nor does she speak of the doctrine of the Trinity, although the brief compass of her article does not allow for comprehensiveness.

once poor pagans. . . . It is just not true that the significance of Jesus is only eschatological and not historical.[89]

And it is because Jesus, as only a Jew could, opened the one
covenant of salvation to all men and women that he stands at
the center of Christian life. For the Gentile Christian, then,
Jesus is "the Second Abraham, the one who is uniquely its Pa-
triarch."[90] Thus the Jews are not those who repudiated their
own Messiah; rather "the Jewish non-acceptance of Jesus as the
Christ is an act of faithfulness to the God of the covenant, and
not, as in the historical Christian polemics, an act of faithlessness."[91]

Thus Eckardt holds that Jesus partially fulfilled messianic
expectations insofar as the pagans were brought into salvation.
He does not claim that all men are to acknowledge Jesus as
Messiah and Lord. Within the one covenant of God with his
people, there will continue a dialectical tension between Judaism and Christianity until the end of time. Each has a vocation to the world and to one another—to announce the revelation which God has given in their respective histories, the events
of Israel's history no less revelatory and final than those of
Christians.

Cornelius A. Rijk, one-time head of the Vatican office on
Catholic-Jewish relations, sees as potentially fruitful and benefi-
cial the perennial tension between those who think the Messiah
has come and those who do not think so. Christians must re-
shape what they mean by "Messiah" in the face of the obvious
non-realization of the messianic age in history, although, in
some way, Messiah was realized in Jesus.[92] "Jesus . . . really
and entirely fulfilled the covenant in the deepest sense of the
word. . . . But not all the dimensions of Jesus' messiahship had

89. A. Roy Eckardt, "Comments at Israel Study Group," p. 2.

90. *Idem, Elder Brother*, p. 159.

91. *Idem*, "Toward an Authentic Jewish-Christian Relationship," p. 277;
cf. also *idem*, "End to the Christian Jewish Dialogue."

92. Cornelius A. Rijk, "The Holy Year and Reconciliation Between Christians and Jews," *SIDIC* 7, #3 (1974):21-23 (p. 23); cf. *idem*, "Some Observations," pp. 3-17.

yet been revealed."[93] This new covenant fulfilled in Jesus does not inaugurate a second covenant; rather it renews the old covenant, while God continues to cherish the people who understand their faithfulness to that covenant by not accepting Jesus as its fulfillment. God is faithful to his people and to his promises. And so, like Eckardt, Rijk recognizes both continuity and discontinuity in the relation between Judaism and Christianity. Both Christianity and Judaism, in their complementary witness to the "already" and "not yet" of the messianic age, act on God's will in bringing about the Kingdom of God:

> The difference between them consists fundamentally in the realized eschatology in Christ which has created a unique situation. Christians are linked to, are baptized into, this eschatological event, but they must extend its meaning and its historical dimensions to the whole of human history, in time and space. Jews, on the other hand, remaining faithful to their revealed heritage, and being thus a blessing for mankind, witnessing to the 'not yet' of the entire messianic age, force Christians to become more vividly aware of the dimensions of the final eschatological event.[94]

C.
AN OVERVIEW

While inconsistencies of categorical identification make one chary about noting trends of theologies/Christologies of discontinuity and continuity, certain drifts nevertheless emerge from Christologies which stress one or the other. Without identifying any thinker with one, all, or a combination of these, one can see a certain pattern of Christological/ecclesiological/soteriological doctrines forming (of course, many of these are a matter of emphasis rather than mutually exclusive tenets):

93. *Idem*, "Some Observations," pp. 11f; see also *idem*, "Ecumenism and Dialogue" *SIDIC* 1, #3 (1968):15-17 (p. 16).
94. *Idem*, "Some Observations," p. 14; see also *idem*, "Catholics and Jews after 1967," on the dialectical relation between Judaism and Christianity. Quoted by permission.

Theologians of Discontinuity Stress:	*Theologians of Continuity Stress:*
Uniqueness and finality of Christ	Relativity of Christ; the "function" of Christ in Christian consciousness
Jesus is Messiah; fulfilled the hopes of the Jewish people and the prophecies of the Old Testament	Jesus is Messiah proleptically, only in the end times; Messianic times not yet but to be realized by the Church and Judaism in history
Christ is absolute fulfillment of Jewish faith and Scripture	Christ is partial fulfillment of Jewish faith and Scripture
Jesus Christ is divine, second person of the Trinity	Jesus Christ is divine, but have to understand the content of that statement in the face of the nature of religious language and in the context of how all men share divinity
Mystery of Jewish "no"; God in his mercy is faithful to his people despite their rejection of Christ	Positive evaluation of Jewish "no"; Jews' faithful response to their covenant and to their understanding of messianic fulfillment
Christianity successor to Judaism; Judaism preparatory to Christianity; Christianity as the New Chosen People	Continuing validity of Judaism alongside Christianity, not (only) in preparation to; expressed in terms of: a. schism theology: complementary witness of Judaism and Christianity b. two covenants
Missionary exigence to preach Christ to all men, including Jews	Obligation to witness to one's belief, acknowledge place of Christ in one's religious consciousness, but no exigency to convert Jews—conversion a matter of calling all persons to faithfulness within the revelation God has gifted them with

IV
Conclusions

In the last thirty-five years, a host of factors have pushed Christians into a rethinking of their portrayal of Jews in their catechetics and popular preaching.[1] Similarly, Christians have examined anew how Christianity is related to Judaism and reflected about the abiding validity of Judaism, and about how Christian theology leaves room for, or encroaches upon, that validity. It is primarily within the last decade that these latter themes have received focused and conscious attention from Christian denominations and thinkers. In our study we have outlined prevailing Christological trends of the Christian Churches and thinkers in their newly-assumed dialogical posture vis-à-vis Judaism, and we have noticed that these trends, while rooted in Christology, are also closely tied to, and sometimes functions of, soteriology and ecclesiology.

1. Most notable have been the numerous studies on antisemitic trends in Christian catechetical materials. The literature on this subject is quite extensive; we mention a few here: "Bad Schwalbach: Proposals for Christian Religious Teaching, 1950," *SIDIC* 3 (1970):#2:5-7; Claire Huchet Bishop, *How Catholics Look at Jews: Inquiries into Italian, Spanish, and French Teaching Materials* (New York: Paulist Press, 1974); Paul Diemann and R. Bloch, *Catéchèse chrétienne et peuple de la Bible* (Paris: Cahiers Sions, 1952); Charles Y. Glock and Rodney Stark, *Christian Beliefs and Anti-Semitism* (New York: Harper and Row, 1966); Bruce Long, *Judaism and the Christian Seminary Curriculum* (Chicago: Loyola University Press, 1966); F. Lovsky, *Le Peuple d-Israël dans l-education chrétienne* (Paris: Societe des Ecoles du dimanche, 1971); Bernhard Olson, *Faith and Prejudice: Intergroup Problems in Protestant Curricula* (New Haven: Yale University Press, 1972); John T. Pawlikowski, *Catechetics and Prejudice: How Catholic Teaching Materials View Jews, Protestants, and Racial Minorities* (New York: Paulist Press, 1973); *idem*, "Christian-Jewish Relations and Catholic Teaching Materials," *Catholic Library World* 45 (1973):227-232; Gerald Strober, *Portrait of the Elder Brother: Jews and Judaism in Protestant Teaching Materials* (New York: NCCJ/AJC, 1972).

We have tried to refrain from a "running" evaluation of these Christologies, although value-laden adjectives like "progressive," "contradictory," "absolutist," etc., have crept into our primarily descriptive analysis. Sometimes, too, our categorizing a theologian within a particular group has obscured the nuances which properly accrue to a full, worked-out Christology, but such associating may be as unavoidable as it is misleading in such a study. We have striven for comprehensiveness perhaps at the expense of incisiveness, yet the many ways this issue may be treated—through notions of election, covenant, Christology, ecclesiology, missiology, soteriology—justifies, we think, this course of action. It is now time to make some general observations.

Initial Christological proposals can be only provisional because of the incipient character of the Jewish-Christian dialogue. There has not yet been time for theologians to assess one another's work on this topic, or even to narrow the issue enough to reflect thematically upon it. Indeed it is as if the starting gate were thrown open, and each person/Church has raced down the track without opportunity yet to look at, and assess, the track performance of the other contestants. Perhaps our study has thrown light on common themes which will integrate and sharpen Christological reflection in the future. From our viewpoint, some of these reflections might go in the following direction.

Eva Marie Fleischner notes that a pluralism of Christologies exists already within the New Testament (see the previous chapter), to say nothing of within the Christological development after apostolic times. Doctrinal pluralism is a relatively new thematic consideration for the Christian Church, but its importance and ramifications are being noted more and more. A properly worked-out theology of pluralism[2] may provide the most fruitful method of approaching our problem. Admittedly this complicates an already crowded theological agenda, but the

---

2. By "properly worked-out" we mean a theology which takes into account the nature of religious language, the history of Christian theology, the biblical witness, and the presence and validity of other world religions.

importance of theological pluralism lies in the fact that Judaism, like Christianity, is a complex, multi-faceted reality, affected too by its own theological pluralism. Christians have as often as not oversimplified their position vis-à-vis Judaism when they have made sweeping assertions that Judaism believes this or that.

Bernard Lonergan, in considering doctrinal pluralism, has noted that "something can be understood only within a certain context." Conversely a new context provides for, and often necessitates, a new understanding. Because contexts change, a fear of rampant relativism may make one shirk off working through a new understanding[3]—or even deny that a new understanding is possible or needed. Nevertheless, the presence of the new context outlined in Chapter I of this study illustrates the need and opportunity for a new Christian understanding of its belief in Christ.

Religious pluralism is a fact that Christians must explain to themselves in the light of their belief in the universal efficacy of Christ. But pluralism is not a good in itself. If it were, then it would be incumbent upon Christians to spread it by encouraging a multiplication of religions. Confronted by the fact of pluralism, then, some form of logos-Christology may prove most fruitful as a way for *Christians* to recognize the validity of other religions (and, *a fortiori*, of Judaism). Karl Rahner employs logos-Christology as a way of working out a Christology in the face of the plurality of religions,[4] and the success of this effort with regard to leaving theological room for Judaism has been

---

3. As John B. Cobb notes: "The apparent danger of pluralism is that it leads to a debilitating relativism. If pluralism relativizes all traditions, it seems to imply that because they are equally good our own choice of values or meanings is arbitrary.... The threat of relativism is the most critical issue the Christian has to face." From *Christ in a Pluralistic Age,* by John B. Cobb, Jr. Copyright 1975 The Westminster Press, p. 58f. Used by Permission.

4. Cf. Karl Rahner, "Current Problems in Christology," in *Theological Investigations* (Baltimore: Helicon Press, 1961), I:149-154; *idem*, "Theology of the Incarnation," *Theological Investigations* (Baltimore: Helicon Press, 1966), IV:105-120.

noted by Eugene Borowitz.[5] Interestingly enough, recent, but very different, Christological studies by John Cobb and David Tracy have noted the usefulness and compatibility of the logos tradition for constructing a Christology which respects, and accounts for, pluralism in religion from a *Christian* point of view.[6] Our study cannot evaluate these recent attempts, nor, much less, outline in more detail a Christology fully worked out in the context of the Jewish-Christian dialogue. This would require another full study. But it can at least be said that logos-Christology, properly understood, does not see Judaism as only preparatory to Christianity, as destined to disappear from the earth. Rather it sees Judaism as one of God's ways of speaking to his world through his continued election of the Jewish people in terms which *Christians* can understand. Logos-Christology does not dictate a Christian self-understanding to Jews. Both Peter Chirico and Eva Fleischner have shown the deleterious effects which follow from a propositional understanding of revelation and have indicated how an incarnational notion of revelation mediates the clash between Judaism and Christianity—which notion logos-Christology illustrates.

The Christian does claim, however, a vision of truth. It is a vision he is committed to talk about, one that he treasures, and one that he may share. This vision, more and more Christians

---

5. Rabbi Eugene B. Borowitz, "Contemporary Christologies: A Jewish Response" (Paper presented at the meeting of the American Theological Society, New York City, April 1975), p. 123, agrees that Rahner's Christology may provide the best arena for Jewish-Christian dialogue. Further, Avery Dulles, "Response to Rabbi Eugene Borowitz' 'Contemporary Christologies' " (Paper given at the American Theological Society, New York City, April 1975), p. 4, agrees that Rahner's (and Tillich's) notion of symbol may provide a fruitful contact point between the faiths, while avoiding some pitfalls of liberal theology.

6. Cf. John Cobb, *Christ in a Pluralistic Age*, pp. 31-94, especially pp. 58ff; David Tracy, *Blessed Rage for Order: The New Pluralism in Theology* (New York: The Seabury Press, 1975), pp. 204ff. On p. 206, Tracy contrasts "exclusivist" Christology (a christocentrism which holds "that only and solely God's 'special revelation' in Jesus Christ is meaningful for a proper human self-understanding") and "inclusivist" Christology. As a foundation for the latter, Tracy cites Rahner's notions of revelation (similar to Chirico's mentioned below), implicit Christianity, and salvation history (cf. also Tracy, pp. 225f, fn. 20). Tracy claims that it is this tradition of an inclusivist Christology which informs his own formulation, although he thinks Rahner has not gone far enough in working out its implications (cf. Tracy, p. 217).

are coming to see, *includes* the validity and value of the Jewish faith in itself and of the Hebrew Scriptures in themselves *and* as preparatory to Christian faith in Christ. For the Christian to eliminate the preparatory character as *a* valid way to understand the Hebrew Scriptures would be to remove the anchor which gives Christianity any validity and would open it to the a-historical temptations of Gnosticism and Docetism. The Christian debt to Judaism is not only for *their* sacred books and for *their* interpretation, but also for the Christian savior and for the Christian interpretation of that savior.

A theological pluralism, fleshed out by a logos-Christology which would grant and account for a Christ who is Messiah for Christians and for the abiding validity of the Jewish tradition for Jews, may, in the end, bring about a new rapprochement between Jew and Christian. This theological pluralism would reflect more accurately, too, the many and varied ways that God has spoken and does speak to his people.

*   *   *   *   *

A factor which emerges after one surveys the recent history of the Jewish-Christian encounter is the profound way that the posture of dialogue has affected the content of what Christians are saying about their belief in Christ. Admittedly Christians of a fundamentalist persuasion have not been as eager as mainline and liberal Christians to enter into dialogue, but of those who have, we have noticed how their language about Jesus is less absolutist, their claims about messianic fulfillment less univocal.

One should be cautious, however, not to exaggerate the impact of this Christological trend on Christian theology throughout the world. For, as Hans Weber notes, the Jewish-Christian dialogue is a primarily North Atlantic affair.[7] Nevertheless the developments and progress of the dialogue should not be, on that account, minimized.

That the Jewish-Christian dialogue has concentrated its activity in one part of the world points up an important consideration for its participants—namely, what are its implications on

---

7. Hans Ruedi Weber, "Jewish-Christian Dialogue: A North Atlantic Affair?" *The Ecumenical Review* 25 (1973):216-221.

the dialogue with non-Christian religions other than Judaism? As many Jews have become quite wary of the possibility of a "super-Christian Church" emerging from the ecumenical movement, one might speculate that members of other religions might wonder whether, in the face of a new rapprochement between Christianity and Judaism, there is "theological room" for non-biblical, non-salvationist religions of the world. In other words, is the emphasis on the common patrimony of Christians and Jews, "two equal vocations within the one people of God," or even the Jews' special, pre-eminent place in current salvation history going to present the same dilemma (affirming the validity of other religious expressions) to a Jewish-Christian coalition? Again, a theological pluralism, mediated through a logos-Christology, may be the most fruitful way for *Christians* to validate and account for other religions.[8]

Some Christian spokespersons, noting the Christian effort to reformulate its doctrines about Christ in less absolutist terms, suggest that the time may be right for Jews to re-evaluate their understanding/estimation of Jesus, not only in order to understand the place Jesus holds in Christians' consciousness, but also in order to rethink the place Jesus may have in their own tradition.[9] Furthermore, the Jewish-Christian dialogue has matured to the point where Jewish scholars are beginning to note and comment upon the pluralism of Christian theology.

8. On this very issue, see Raymond Pannikar, "Christians and So-Called 'Non-Christians,'" *Cross Currents* 22 (1973):281-308. Pannikar's position is related to Rahner's logos-Christology, but his own creative twist to it, combined with his considerable knowledge of world religions, merits closer attention than it has received.

9. In recent years, there has been a renaissance of Jewish interest in Jesus and the way Jesus is presented in Jewish teaching materials. E.g., Robert Aron, *The Jewish Jesus* (Maryknoll, N.Y.: Orbis Books, 1971); Shalom Ben-Chorin, "The Image of Jesus in Modern Judaism," *JES* 11 (1974):410-430; Gustaf Dalman, *Jesus-Jeshua: Studies in the Gospels* (New York: KTAV Publishing House, 1971); David Flusser, *Jesus* (New York: Herder and Herder, 1969); Morris Goldstein, *Jesus in the Jewish Tradition* (New York: The Macmillan Co., 1950); S. Katz, "Christology: A Jewish view," *Scottish Journal of Theology* 24 (1971):184-200; Pinchos Lapide, "Learning about Jesus—in Israel," *The Ecumenical Review* 25 (1973):221-228; J. Rabbi Riemer, "Teaching about Non-Jews in Jewish Schools," *Catholic Mind* 72 (March 1974):43-51; Samuel Sandmel, *We Jews and Jesus* (New York: Oxford University Press, 1965); Geza Vermes, *Jesus the Jew* (London: Collins, 1973).

Germane to our concern of Christology is the quite remarkable and insightful paper by Eugene Borowitz, "Contemporary Christologies: A Jewish Response."[10]

Eugene Borowitz notes that the problem of inter-religious dialogue is as often a matter of different epistemological positions as it is a matter of different faith perspectives. With less precise language we have noted this same difficulty with regard to evangelicals who, as a matter of principle, cannot assume a posture of dialogue without including a missionary stance; nor can they admit that Christ is not the absolute fulfillment of Old Testament prophecies. Borowitz points out that there may be as much of a chasm between such persons and liberal theologians as between Christian and Jew: "Traditionalists and liberals speak from different standards of truth."

> For a liberal of one faith to criticize a traditionalist of another faith, or vice versa, is, properly speaking, not to have an inter-religious discussion at all. . . . The fundamental difference here is not the content of the two faiths —which one would take to be the proper substance of inter-religious discussions on the level of engaged disagreement—but between the different ways of apprehending religious truth. . . . Thus, in the case of the resurrection, there is as good as no difference between liberal Jews and liberal Christians in evaluating the adequacy of traditionalist Christian arguments for its historicity. The same is true with a whole range of assertions in traditional christologies.[11]

Borowitz, in evaluating the Christologies of prominent Christian thinkers, concludes that Rosemary Ruether's assertion that antisemitism is the left-hand of Christology is not fully accurate:

> . . . classic christology was closely associated with anti-Semitism and while some remnants of it are to be found

10. See fn. 5 in this chapter.
11. Eugene Borowitz, "Contemporary Christologies," p. 47. Quoted by permission.

among traditionalist [Christian] theologians, other tradi-
tionalists as well as liberals [e.g., Schoonenberg, Soelle,
Ruether] and post-liberals [e.g., Rahner] have found anti-
Semitism antithetical to their understanding of Christ.
They have therefore eliminated it from their teaching.[12]

Even if Ruether's thesis is not fully and necessarily accurate, her historical investigations demonstrate that more often
than not the backwash from Christian absolutist claims, however, spell out grave implications for the Christian mission.[13] In
Chapter III we have seen that the missionary exigence vis-à-vis
the Jew flows primarily from one's ecclesiological, not Christological, position. Not to underestimate the intrinsic relation between Christology and ecclesiology, a possibly fruitful avenue
for future dialogues may be to evaluate how different ecclesiologies are more or less supersessionist. For those who find salvation given in and through Jesus of Nazareth, what model best
elucidates the community which has formed after him but which
leaves room for those who hear God's call through the Hebrew
religion? This, of course, is matter enough for another thesis.
We mention the missiological question here only because it
flows from a consideration of Christology in the Jewish-Christian encounter.

Christology, as Christianity itself, is open to, and in need
of, constant revision. Because revelation stands before us as well
as behind us, Christian insight into its own mystery stands within an ever widening horizon. The fear of tampering with doc-

12. *Ibid.*, p. 124. Borowitz maintains that, while liberal theology "remains
congenial to Jews" (p. 121), there are some characteristics inherent to liberalism
which are harmful to both Judaism and Christianity. In the liberal view, "How
does one deal with the symbols of uniqueness in a faith that no longer affirms
it? . . . How much reinterpretation can a symbol [here, Christ] receive and still
retain its authenticity? . . . Why maintain a separate community and the bur-
dens of a special tradition if there are no essential differences between them?"
(p. 66; cf. also pp. 65, 53). Quoted by permission. See also Avery Dulles, "Response," on this same point.
13. Indeed, the posture of dialogue in the Roman Catholic Church since
Vatican II has caused the major Roman Catholic religious order concerned with
the mission to the Jews—the Sisters of Sion—to re-evaluate its service in the
Church. See Sr. Celia Deutsch, "Sion's Mission in the Church" (Toronto,
1974).

trines and viewpoints that have been handed down through the ages may be somewhat calmed when it is realized that the God of Abraham, who is the God of Jesus, is the same faithful God who speaks to his people and draws them forward to that final day. And it may just turn out that the rethinking of Christian belief in Jesus, in the face of the abiding validity of Judaism, will turn into an ever-deepening, rather than a shallow, expression of their faith. We think that our survey has been evidence that such can result from the Jewish-Christian dialogue.

Bibliography

Aagard, Johannes. "The Church and the Jews in Eschatology." *Lutheran World* 11 (1964):270-278.

Abbott, Walter, ed. *The Documents of Vatican II*. New York: Association Press, 1966.

Agus, Jacob. *Dialogue and Tradition: The Challenges of Contemporary Judaeo-Christian Thought*. New York: Abelard-Schuman, 1971.

————. "Israel and the Jewish-Christian Dialogue." *Journal of Ecumenical Studies* [hereafter *JES*] 6 (1969):18-36.

————. "Revelation as Quest—A Contribution to Ecumenical Thought." *JES* 9 (1972):521-543.

Althouse, La Vonne. *When Jew and Christian Meet*. New York: Friendship Press, 1966.

"American Lutheran Church and the Jewish Community," in *1974 Reports and Actions: Seventh General Convention of the American Lutheran Church*, pp. 752-757.

Aron, Robert. *The Jewish Jesus*. Maryknoll, N.Y.: Orbis Books, 1971.

"Bad Schwalbach: Proposals for Christian Religious Teaching. 1950." *Service International de Documentation Judéo-Chrétienne* [hereafter *SIDIC*] 3 (1970)#2:5-7.

Balthasar, Hans urs Von. *Church and World*. New York: Herder and Herder, 1967.

Barth, Markus. *Israel and the Church: Contribution to a Dialogue Vital for Peace*. Richmond, Va.: John Knox Press, 1969.

————. "Salvation from the Jews?" *JES* 1 (1964):323-326.

————. "Was Paul an Anti-Semite?" *JES* 5 (1968):78-104.

Baum, Gregory. *Commentary on the Second Vatican Council's Declaration on the Relation of the Church to Non-Christian Religions*. London: Centre for Biblical Jewish Studies, n.d.

————. "The Doctrinal Basis for Jewish-Christian Dialogue." *The Month* 224 (1967).232-245.

————. "Introduction" to Rosemary Ruether's *Faith and Fratricide: The Theological Roots of Anti-Semitism*. New York: The Seabury Press, 1974.

————. *Is the New Testament Anti-Semitic? A Re-Examination of the New Testament*. New York: Paulist Press, 1965.

————. "The Jews, Faith and Ideology." *The Ecumenist* 10 (1971-1972):71-76.

————. "Theology After Auschwitz: A Conference Report." *The Ecumenist* 12 (1974):65-80.

Bea, Augustine Cardinal. *The Church and the Jewish People.* London: Geoffrey Chapman, 1966.

————. "Commentary on 'Declaration of the Church's Relations with Non-Christian Religions.'" *SIDIC* #1 (1967):4.

Berkhof, H. "Israel as a Theological Problem in the Christian Church." *JES* 6 (1969):329-347.

Berkovits, Eliezer. *Faith After the Holocaust.* New York: KTAV Publishing House, 1973.

Birmingham, William. "Judaism: Can Christians Say It Is Real?" *The Lamp* 67 (January 1969):23ff.

Bishop, Claire Huchet. *How Catholics Look at Jews: Inquiries into Italian, Spanish, and French Teaching Materials.* New York: Paulist Press, 1974.

Bokser, Ben Zion. *Judaism and the Christian Predicament.* New York: Alfred A. Knopf, 1967.

Borowitz, Eugene B. "Contemporary Christologies: A Jewish Response." Paper Presented at the Meeting of the American Theological Society, New York City, April 1975.

Bowler, Maurice. "Rosenzweig on Judaism and Christianity—The Two Covenant Theory." *Judaism* 22 (1973):475-481.

Bratton, Fred Gladstone. *The Crime of Christendom: The Theological Sources of Christian Anti-Semitism.* Boston: Beacon Press, 1969.

Buber, Martin. *Two Types of Faith.* London: Routledge and Kegan Paul, Ltd., 1951.

Catanzaro, C. J. de. "The Meaning of Prophecy." In *Jews and Christians: Preparation for Dialogue*, pp. 57-65. Edited by George A. F. Knight. Philadelphia: Westminster Press, 1965.

Cerfaux, Lucien. *The Church in the Theology of St. Paul.* New York: Herder, 1959.

Chirico, Peter. "Christian and Jew Today from a Theological Perspective." *JES* 7 (1970):744-762.

Chorin, Shalom Ben-. "The Image of Jesus in Modern Judaism." *JES* 11 (1974):410-430.

Chouraqui, Andre, and Daniélou, Jean. *The Jews: Views and Counterviews—A Dialogue.* New York: Paulist Press, 1967.

"Christian-Jewish Relations at the Diocesan Synod of Vienna—October 3, 1970." *Encounter Today* 6 (1971):95-97.

"The Church and the Jewish People—1964, 1969." *Speaking of God Today: Jews and Lutherans in Dialogue*, pp. 166-173. Edited by Paul Opsahl and Marc C. Tanenbaum. Philadelphia: Fortress Press, 1974.

Cobb, John B., Jr., *Christ in a Pluralistic Age.* Philadelphia: The Westminster Press, 1975.

Cross, Frank M. "A Christian Understanding of the Election of Israel." In *The Death of Dialogue and Beyond*, pp. 72-85. Edited by Sanford Seltzer and Max L. Stackhouse. New York: Friendship Press, 1969.

Crossan, Dominic M. "Anti-Semitism and the Gospel." *Theological Studies* 26 (1965):189-214.

Cushing, Richard Cardinal. "Commentary on the 'Declaration of the Church's Relations with Non-Christian Religions.'" *SIDIC* #1 (1967):4.

Cushman, Robert E. "Biblical Election as Sacred History: A Study in the Ancient History of Ecumenism." In *Our Common History as Christians: Essays in Honor of Albert C. Outler*, pp. 179-216. Edited by John Deschner *et al.* New York: Oxford University Press, 1975.

Dahl, Nils A. "Election and the People of God." *Lutheran Quarterly* 21 (1969):430-436.

―――. "Election and the People of God: Some Comments." In *Speaking of God Today: Jews and Lutherans in Dialogue*, pp. 31-38. Edited by Paul Opsahl and Marc C. Tanenbaum. Philadelphia: Fortress Press, 1974.

Dalman, Gustaf. *Jesus-Jeshua: Studies in the Gospels.* New York: KTAV Publishing House, 1971.

Daniélou, Jean. *The Dead Sea Scrolls and Primitive Christianity.* Baltimore: Helicon Press, 1958.

―――. *Dialogue Avec Israël.* Paris: La Palatine, 1963.

―――. *The Theology of Jewish Christianity.* Chicago: Henry Regnery Co., 1964.

Davies, Alan T. *Anti-Semitism and the Christian Mind: The Crisis of Conscience after Auschwitz.* New York: Herder and Herder, 1969.

―――. "The Jews in an Ecumenical Context: A Critique." *JES* 5 (1968):488-506.

Davies, W. D. "Christianity and Judaism." In *The Jewish Heritage Reader.* Edited by Lily Edelman. New York: Taplinger Publishing Co., 1965.

―――. "Torah and Dogma: A Comment―." In *The Death of Dialogue and Beyond*, pp. 120-144. Edited by Sanford Seltzer and Max L. Stackhouse. New York: Friendship Press, 1969.

Dawidowicz, Lucy S. *The War Against the Jews, 1933-1945.* New York: Holt, Rinehart, and Winston, 1975.

"De Judaeis: The Original and Revised Versions." *The Tablet* 218 (1964):1093f.

De Corneille, Roland. *Christians and Jews: The Tragic Past and the Hopeful Future.* Toronto: Longmans Canada, Ltd., 1966.

Demann, Paul, and Bloch, R. *Catéchèse chrétienne et peuple de la Bible.* Paris: Cahiers Sions, 1952.

Deutsch, Sr. Celia. "Sion's Mission in the Church." Charter of the Sisters of Sion. Toronto, 1975. (mimeograph)

Dulles, Avery. "Response to Rabbi Eugene Borowitz' 'Contemporary Christologies.' " Paper given at the American Theological Society, New York City, April 1975. (xerox)

Dupont, Jacques. "Un Dossier sur diverses options exégétiques et théologiques concernant Israël." *Foi et Vie* 5 (1967):51-84.

Eckardt, A. Roy. *Christianity and the Children of Israel: A Theological Approach to the Jewish Question.* New York: King's Crown Press, 1948.

–––––. "Comments at Israel Study Group Meeting, April 5, 1975, on Rosemary Ruether's FAITH AND FRATRICIDE." New York City. (xerox)

–––––. "The Contemporary Jewish-Christian Encounter in North America." Paper Presented at the International Conference of Christians and Jews, York University, Toronto, September 2-6, 1968. (mimeograph)

–––––. *Elder and Younger Brothers: The Encounter of Jews and Christians.* New York: Charles Scribner's Sons, 1967.

–––––. "End to the Christian-Jewish Dialogue." *Christian Century* 83 (1966):393-395.

–––––. "Toward an Authentic Jewish-Christian Relationship." *Journal of Church and State* 13 (1971):271-282.

–––––. *Your People, My People.* New York: Quadrangle, 1974.

Eckardt, Alice. "The Holocaust: Jewish and Christian Responses." *Journal of the American Academy of Religion* 42 (1974):453-469.

Eckert, W. P. "Messianism and the Church." *Encounter Today* 4 (1969):21-29.

Estes, Joseph R. "Jewish-Christian Dialogue as Mission." *Review and Expositor* 68 (1971):5-16.

"The Evanston Report (1954)." *Lutheran World* 11 (1964):358.

Filthaut, Theodor. *Israel in der Christlichen Unterweisung.* Munich: Koesel Verlag, 1963.

Fitzmyer, Joseph. "Anti-Semitism and the Cry of All the Peoples." *Theological Studies* 26 (1965):667-671.

Flannery, Edward. *The Anguish of the Jews.* New York: Macmillan Co., 1964.

–––––. "The Church, the Synagogue, and the Ecumenical Movement." *Catholic Theological Society of America Proceedings* 21 (1966):315-322.

–––––. "Jesus, Israel, and the Christian Renewal." *JES* 9 (1972):418-450.

Fleischner, Eva Marie. "The Religious Significance of Israel: A Christian Perspective." In *Jewish-Christian Relations*, pp. 17-25. Edited by Robert Heyer. New York: Paulist Press, 1975.

————. *Judaism in German Christian Theology Since 1945: Christianity and Israel Considered In Terms of Mission.* ATLA Monograph #8. Metuchen, N.J.: The Scarecrow Press Inc. 1975.

Flusser, David. *Jesus.* New York: Herder and Herder, 1969.

————. "A New Sensitivity in Judaism and the Christian Message." *Encounter Today* 4 (1969):123-133.

Gartenhaus, Jacob. "How To Approach the Jew with the Gospel." *Christianity Today* 11 (1966):253-255.

Gilbert, Arthur. *The Vatican Council and the Jews.* New York: World Publishing Co., 1968.

Glatzer, Nahum (presenter). *Franz Rosenzweig: His Life and Thought.* New York: Schocken Books, 1953.

Glock, Charles Y., and Stark, Rodney. *Christian Beliefs and Anti-Semitism.* New York: Harper and Row, 1966.

Goldstein, Morris. *Jesus in the Jewish Tradition.* New York: The Macmillan Co., 1950.

Goppelt, Leonhard. "Israel and the Church in Today's Discussion and in Paul." *Lutheran World* 10 (1963):352-372.

Grant, Frederick C. *Ancient Judaism and the New Testament.* New York: The Macmillan Co., 1959.

Greenberg, Blu. "Report of a Jewish Teacher." *The Ecumenist* 12 (1974):84-86.

"Guidelines and Suggestions for Implementing the Conciliar Declaration '*Nostra Aetate.*' " Commission for Religious Relations with Jews, 1975. In *Jewish-Christian Relations*, pp. 75-82. Edited by Robert Heyer. New York: Paulist Press, 1975.

Harter, William H. "A Methodology for the Analysis of Texts Used in 'Displacement Theologies.' " Paper, 1974.

Heilwig, Monika. "Christian Theology and the Covenant of Israel." *JES* 7 (1970):37-51.

————. "Proposal Towards a Theology of Israel as a Religious Community Contemporary with the Christian." Ph.D. dissertation, Catholic University of America, 1968.

————. "Why We Still Can't Talk." In *Jewish/Christian Relations*, pp. 26-31. Edited by Robert Heyer. New York: Paulist Press, 1975.

Hoffmann, R. "Conversion and the Mission of the Church." *JES* 5 (1968):1-20.

Hollis, Christopher. "Catholic-Jewish Dialogue." Paper presented at the International Conference of Christians and Jews, York University, Toronto, September 2-6, 1968.

————. "The Vatican Council and the Jews." *Dublin Review* 241 (1967):24-39.

Horbury, William. "Jesus the Jew." *Theology* 77 (1974):227-232.

Hruby, Kurt. "Israël, peuple de Dieu: exist-t-il une théologie d'Israël dans l'Eglise" *Lumiére et Vie* 18 (1969):59-82.
————. "Jesus, Disciple of Moses: The True Relationship of Christianity and Judaism." *Encounter Today* 8 (1972):4-10.
————. "Peoplehood in Judaism and Christianity." *Theology Digest* 22 (1974):3-12.
————. "Reflections on the Dialogue." In *Brothers in Hope*, pp. 106-131. Edited by John M. Oesterreicher. New York: Herder and Herder, 1970.
"Introduction to the Discussions of the Plenary Session," Meeting on How To Implement the Conciliar Declaration *Nostra Aetate*, No. 4. *SIDIC* 3 (1970):#2:22-24.
Isaac, Jules. *Jesus and Israel.* New York: Holt, Rinehart, and Winston, 1971.
————. *The Teaching of Contempt: Christian Roots of Anti-Semitism.* New York: Holt, Rinehart, and Winston, 1964.
"Jewish-Christian Dialogue: Bridge in Hope." Commission on Ecumenical Affairs, United Methodist General Conference, 1972." *SIDIC* 6 (1973):#3:36-37.
Jocz, Jacob. *Christians and Jews: Encounter and Mission.* London: SPCK, 1966.
————. *The Jewish People and Jesus Christ: A Study in the Controversy Between Church and Synagogue.* London: SPCK, 1954 [revised from 1949].
————. *A Theology of Election: Israel and the Church.* London: SPCK, 1958.
Katz, S. "Christology: A Jewish View." *Scottish Journal of Theology* 24 (1971):184-200.
Klein, Charlotte, "The Theological Dimensions of the State of Israel." *JES* 10 (1973):700-715.
Klick, Cora. "Are You He Who Is To Come?" *Lutheran Quarterly* 24 (1972):51-65.
Knight, George A. F. "Building Theological Bridges: I. The Incarnation." In *Jews and Christians: Preparation for Dialogue*, pp. 110-137. Edited by George A. F. Knight. Philadelphia: The Westminster Press, 1965.
————. "Beyond Dialogue." In *Jews and Christians: Preparation for Dialogue*, pp. 165-184. Edited by George A. F. Knight. Philadelphia: The Westminster Press, 1965.
————. "The 'Mystery' of Israel." In *Jews and Christians: Preparation for Dialogue*, pp. 36-56. Edited by George A. F. Knight. Philadelphia: The Westminster Press, 1965.
Lambert, Bernard. *Le Problem oecumenique.* Paris: Centurion, Vol. II, 1962.
Lapide, Pinchos. "Learning about Jesus—in Israel." *The Ecumenical Review* 25 (1973):221-228.

Laurentin, Rene. *Commentary on the Declaration on the Relation of the Church to Non-Christian Religions.* Ramsey, N.J.: Paulist Press, 1966.

Leeming, Bernard. *The Vatican Council and Christian Unity.* New York: Harper and Row, 1966.

Lindsey, R. L. "Salvation and the Jews." *International Review of Missions* 61 (1972):20-37.

Littell, Franklin H. "Christians and Jews and Ecumenism." *Dial* 10 (1971):249-255.

————. "Christendom, Holocaust and Israel: The Importance for Christians of Recent Major Events in Jewish History." *JES* 10 (1973):483-497.

————. *The Crucifixion of the Jews: The Failure of Christians To Understand the Jewish Experience.* New York: Harper and Row, 1975.

Long, Bruce, ed. *Judaism and the Christian Seminary Curriculum.* Chicago: Loyola University Press, 1966.

Louis-Gabriel, Sr. "Christians, Jews, and Ecumenism." *Catholic Mind* 67 (1969):11-20.

Lovsky, F. *Le Peuple d'Israël dans l'education chrétienne.* Paris: Societe des Ecoles du dimanche, 1971.

Mannheim, Karl. *Ideology and Utopia: An Introduction to the Sociology of Knowledge.* New York: Harcourt, Brace and World, Inc., 1936.

Moltmann, Jürgen. *The Crucified God.* New York: Harper and Row, 1974.

Murphy, Roland E. "Present Biblical Scholarship as a Bond of Understanding." In *Torah and Gospel: Jewish and Catholic Theology in Dialogue,* pp. 81-96. Edited by Philip Scharper. New York: Sheed and Ward, 1966.

Mussio, Bishop John King. Address given to a Jewish Congregation in Steubenville, Ohio. *SIDIC* #1 (1967):3-4.

"New York, Rockville Centre and Brooklyn: Guidelines for the Advancement of Catholic-Jewish Relations." *SIDIC* 3 (1970):#2:16-21.

"Noordwijkerhout: Pastoral Recommendations." Plan of Report: "Relations between Jews and Christians." Bishops of the Netherlands, 1970. *SIDIC* 3 (1970):#2:25-32.

O'Collins, Gerald. "Anti-Semitism in the Gospel." *Theological Studies* 26 (1965):663-666.

Olson, Bernhard. *Faith and Prejudice: Intergroup Problems in Protestant Curricula.* New Haven: Yale University Press, 1972.

Oesterreicher, John M. "The Catholic-Jewish Encounter." In *National Catholic Education Association Bulletin* 56 (1969):36-42.

————. "Declaration on the Relationship of the Church to Non-Christian Religions: Introduction and Commentary." In *Commentary on the Documents of Vatican II*, III:1-136. Edited by H. Vorgrimler. New York: Herder and Herder, 1969.

————. "Deicide as a Theological Problem." In *Brothers In Hope*, pp. 190-205. Edited by John M. Oesterreicher. New York: Herder and Herder, 1970.

————. "Ecumenism and the Jews." *The McAuley Lecture, 1968*. West Hartford, Conn.: St. Joseph College, 1969.

————. "Israel's Misstep and her Rise: The Dialectic of God's Saving Design in Rom. 9-11." *The Bible Today* # 12 (1964):768-774.

————. "Jewish, Christian Traditions Allied—Jesus a Jew." *National Catholic Reporter* 11 #26 (April 25, 1975):16-17.

————. *The Rediscovery of Judaism: A Re-Examination of the Conciliar Statement on the Jews*. South Orange, N.J.: Institute of Judaeo-Christian Studies, 1971.

Opsahl, Paul D. "Report on Jewish-Lutheran Conversations in the USA." [mimeograph]. Lutheran Council in the U.S.A. New York, 1973.

————, and Tanenbaum, Marc C. *Speaking of God Today: Jews and Lutherans in Dialogue*. Philadelphia: Fortress Press, 1974.

Pannikar, Raymond. "Christians and so-called 'Non-Christians.' " *Cross Currents* 22 (1973):281-308.

Papademetriou, George C. "Jewish Rite in the Christian Church: Ecumenical Possibility." *Scottish Journal of Theology* 26 (1973):466-487.

Parkes, James. *Antisemitism*. Chicago: Quadrangle Books, 1963.

————. *The Conflict of the Church and the Synagogue: A Study in the Origins of Antisemitism*. London: The Soncino Press, 1934.

————. "End of the Way." *Encounter Today* 2 (1967):#3:90-93.

————. *The Foundations of Judaism and Christianity*. London: Vallentine-Mitchell, 1960.

————. *Judaism and Christianity*. London: Victor Gallancz, Ltd., 1948.

————. "Judaism and the Jewish People in their World Setting at the End of 1973." Pamphlet, distributed by the Canadian Council of Christians and Jews. Toronto: 1974.

————. *Prelude to Dialogue: Jewish-Christian Relationships*. New York: Schocken Books, 1969.

"Pastoral Orientations with Regard to the Attitude of Christians Toward Judaism" Statement issued by the French Catholic Bishops, April 18, 1973. *Catholic Mind* 71 (1973):51-57.

Pawlikowski, John T. *Catechetics and Prejudice: How Catholic Teaching Materials View Jews, Protestants, and Racial Minorities*. New York: Paulist Press, 1973.

————. "Christ and the Jewish-Christian Dialogue: An Evaluation of Contemporary Perspectives." Paper presented at the American Academy of Religion, Washington, D.C., October 26, 1974.

──────. "Christian-Jewish Relations and Catholic Teaching Materials." *Catholic Library World* 45 (1973):227-232.

──────. "Christian-Jewish Relations: The 1974 Agenda." Paper presented at the Christian-Jewish Relations Conference, Trinity College, University of Toronto, November 26, 1974.

──────. "The Church and Judaism: The Thought of James Parkes." *JES* 6 (1969):573-597.

──────. "Issues in Catholic-Jewish Dialogue." *SIDIC* 7 (1974):#2:22-28.

Plaut, W. G., and Baum, Gregory. "Dialogue: Christian Jewish Relations in Today's World" *Religious Education* 69 (1973):132-149.

Poliakon, Leon. *The History of Anti-Semitism* (4 vols.) New York: The Vanguard Press, 1965.

Rahner, Karl. "Christianity and the Non-Christian Religions." In *Theological Investigations* 5:115-134. Baltimore: Helicon Press, 1966.

──────. "Current Problems in Christology." In *Theological Investigations* I:149-200. Baltimore: Helicon Press, 1961.

──────. "The Hermeneutics of Eschatological Assertions." *Theological Investigations* 4:323-346. Baltimore: Helicon Press, 1966.

──────. "Theology of the Incarnation." In *Theological Investigations* IV:105-120. Baltimore: Helicon Press, 1966.

──────, and Friedmann, F. G. "Unbefangenheit und Anspruch." *Stimmen der Zeit* 178 (1966):81-97.

Rengstorf, K. H. "The Place of the Jew in the Theology of the Christian Mission." *Lutheran World* 11 (1964):279-295.

"Report of the Israel Study Group Meeting." LaGuardia Airport, New York City, April 5, 1975.

Richards, H. "Vatican II and the Jews." *Clergy Review* 49 (1964):552-561.

Riemer, J. Rabbi. "Teaching about non-Jews in Jewish Schools." *Catholic Mind* 72 (March, 1974):43-51.

Rijk, Carnelius A. "Catholics and Jews after 1967: A New Situation." *New Blackfriars* 50 (1968):15-26.

──────. "Ecumenism and Dialogue." *SIDIC* 1 (1968):#3:15-17.

──────. "The Holy Year and Reconciliation Between Christians and Jews." *SIDIC* 7 (1974):#3:21-23.

──────. "Some Observations on a Christian Theology of Judaism." *SIDIC* 5 (1972):#1:3-17.

Rivkin, Ellis. "The Meaning of Messiah in Jewish Thought." *Union Seminary Quarterly Review* 26 (1972):383-406.

Rosenstock-Huessy, Eugen. *Judaism Despite Christianity: Letters between Eugen Rosenstock Huessy and Franz Rosenzweig.* Alabama: University of Alabama Press, 1969.

Rosenzweig, Franz. *The Star of Redemption* [translation of the 2nd edition by William Hello]. New York: Holt, Rinehart and Winston, 1970.

Rossi, Angelo Cardinal. Statement from a meeting of the Jewish-Christian Fraternity. *SIDIC* #1 (1967):3-4.

Rubenstein, Richard L. *After Auschwitz, Radical Theology and Contemporary Judaism*. Indianapolis: Bobbs-Merrill, Co., Inc., 1966.

Ruether, Rosemary Radford. *Faith and Fratricide: The Theological Roots of Anti-Semitism*. New York: The Seabury Press, 1974.

———. "An Invitation to Jewish-Christian Dialogue: In What Sense Can We Say that Jesus was 'The Christ'?" *The Ecumenist* 10 (1972):17-24.

———. "Judaism and Christianity: Two Fourth-Century Religions." *Studies in Religion* 2 (1972):1-10

———. *Messiah of Israel and the Cosmic Christ: A Study of the Development of Christology in Judaism and Early Christianity*. Unpublished manuscript. ca. 1972.

———. "Theological Anti-Semitism in the New Testament." *The Christian Century*. 85 (1968):191-196.

Rylaarsdam, J. Coert. "Common Ground and Differences." *Journal of Religion* 43 (1963):261-270.

———. "Jewish-Christian Relationship: The Two Covenants and the Dilemmas of Christology." *JES* 9 (1972):249-270.

Sandmel, Samuel. *We Jews and Jesus*. New York: Oxford University Press, 1965.

Schoeps, Hans Joachim. *The Jewish-Christian Argument: A History of Theologies in Conflict*. London: Faber and Faber [3rd edition], 1963.

Schubert, Kurt. "The People of the Covenant." In *Brothers in Hope*, pp. 132-158. Edited by John M. Oesterreicher. New York: Herder and Herder, 1970.

"Seelisberg: The Report of Commission 3: A Set of Proposals for Christian Religious Teaching." 1947. *SIDIC* 3 (1970):#2:3-4.

Siegel, S. "Election and the People of God: A Jewish Perspective." *Lutheran Quarterly* 21 (1969):437-450.

Siegmann, Henry, "Dialogue with Christians: A Jewish Dilemma." *Judaism* 20 (1971):93-103.

———. "Commentary on Vatican II." *The Dialogue* #34 (1966):4.

Sheerin, John B. "Commentary on the 1975 Guidelines." In *Jewish-Christian Relations*, pp. 83-85. Edited by Robert Heyer. New York: Paulist Press, 1975.

———. "Evaluating the Past in Catholic-Jewish Relations: Lessons for Today." In *Torah and Gospel: Jewish and Catholic Theology in Dialogue*, pp. 23-24. Edited by Philip Scharper. New York: Sheed and Ward, 1966.

Smith, Elwyn A. "The Religious Meaning of the Land of Israel: A

Christian View." *The Dialogue* #37 (1968:13-16.

"Some Observations and Guidelines for Conversations Between Lutherans and Jews." Lutheran Council of U.S.A. In *Speaking of God Today: Jews and Lutherans in Dialogue*, pp. 163-165. Edited by Paul Opsahl and Marc Tanenbaum. Philadelphia: Fortress Press, 1974.

"A Statement to Our Fellow Christians" by a "group of Christian scholars known as the 'Israel Study Group'." from the Commission on Faith and Order of the National Council of Churches and the Secretariat for Catholic Jewish Relations (NCCB) in U.S. *SIDIC* 6 (1973):#3:33-35.

"A Statement on Interreligious Dialogue Between Jews and Christians," adopted by the General Conference of the United Methodist Church, Atlanta, April 1972.

Stendahl, Krister. "Judaism and Christianity: A Plea for a Relationship." *Cross Currents* 17 (1967):445-459.

———. "Judaism and Christianity: Then and Now." In *The Death of Dialogue and Beyond*, pp. 105-119. Edited by Sanford Seltzer and Max L. Stackhouse. New York: Friendship Press, 1969.

Stephanopoulos, Robert G. "Observations on 'A Statement to our Fellow Christians.' " [xerox]

Strober, Gerald. *Portrait of the Elder Brother: Jews and Judaism in Protestant Teaching Materials*. New York: NCCJ/AJC, 1972.

Stransky, Thomas F. "Reflections." *The Dialogue* #34 (1966):8.

Tillich, Paul. *Christianity and the Encounter of World Religions*. New York: Columbia University Press, 1963.

Tracy, David. *Blessed Rage for Order: The New Pluralism in Theology*. New York: The Seabury Press, 1975.

Tumin, Melvin. *An Inventory and Appraisal of Research on American Anti-Semitism*. New York: Freedom Books, 1961.

"United States: Guidelines for Catholic-Jewish Relations." 1967. *SIDIC* 3 (1970):#2:10-13.

Vawter, Bruce. "Are the Gospels Anti-Semitic?" *JES* 5 (1968):473-487.

Vermes, Geza. *Jesus the Jew*. London: Collins, 1973.

Vogel, Manfred. "Is Authentic Jewish-Christian Dialogue Possible?" *Journal of Bible and Religion* 33 (1965): 134.

———. "The Problem of Dialogue Between Judaism and Christianity." *JES* 4 (1967):684-699.

Vorgrimler, Herbert, ed. *Commentary on the Documents of Vatican II* (6 vols.). New York: Herder and Herder, 1967.

Weber, Hans Ruedi. "Jewish-Christian Dialogue: A North Atlantic Affair?" *The Ecumenical Review* 25 (1973):216-221.

Wilder, Amos. "The Church and Israel in the Light of the Election." *Studia Evangelica IV*, pp. 347-357. Edited by R. M. Cross. Berlin, 1968.

————. "The World Council of Churches and Judaism." In *Judaism and the Christian Seminary Curriculum*, pp. 72-84. Edited by J. Bruce Long. Chicago: Loyola University Press, 1966.

Will, James. "A Response to 'A Statement to our Fellow Christians.'" [xerox]

"Working Document." *Catholic Mind* 68 (1970):59-64.

Wyschogrod, Michael. "Israel, the Church, and Election." In *Brothers in Hope*, pp. 79-87. Edited by John M. Oesterreicher. New York: Herder and Herder, 1970.

————. "The Law: Jews and Gentiles," In *Speaking of God Today: Jews and Lutherans in Dialogue*, pp. 3-14. Edited by Paul Opsahl and Marc Tanenbaum. Philadelphia: Fortress Press, 1974.